THE ALAMEDA
The Beautiful Way

Shannon E. Clark
2006

This book contains The History of The Alameda, The Walking Tour of The Alameda, The Hanchett Residence Park Walking History Tour, and Historical Vignettes. Local companies and organizations have generously made donations to sponsor the publication of this book. Each sponsored page provides additional insight into the history of The Alameda. The Alameda Business Association would like to thank each of these organizations for their individual contribution and support.

ISBN: 1-4243-1868-8
ISBN-13: 978-1-4243-1868-1

Printed in the USA by
BR Printers
1855 Dobbin Drive
San Jose, CA 95133

Published by the Alameda Business Association
www.the-alameda.com

Willliam A. Wulf

Acknowledgements

When the Alameda Business Association proposed writing a history of The Alameda, I immediately embraced the idea. History and writing have always been two of my passions. The prospect of researching, writing and designing a history book was a dream "project."

My first exploratory visit was to Leonard McKay. Leonard had been the "dean" of San Jose historians and was widely respected for his knowledge of local history. Leonard's first reaction to the project was, "You know, I don't think anyone has ever written a history of The Alameda." In fact, he seemed very surprised. I now understand his surprise. Over the course of writing this book, I discovered a new perspective on the history of San Jose—a rich, untold story that echoes the history of California itself. The people, the events, and the elevated status of this grand boulevard create a story that should be known to the residents and businesses that call The Alameda home.

I slowly began piecing together the story of The Alameda using the maps, photos, newspaper articles, and scrap files provided by Jim Reed, archivist for the History San José Research Library at Kelley Park. Jim's dedication and ability to uncover the most obscure historical information is simply impressive! I am proud to have worked with William (Bill) Wulf, Los Gatos historian. He was generous with his time, personal collection of photos, artifacts, and extensive knowledge of San Jose history. He is a great storyteller and I greatly enjoyed our numerous discussions about The Alameda. Historian Charlene Duval brings pure excitement to her study of local history. For Charlene, putting an undiscovered historical connection together based on a newly discovered photo is the same as scoring a fourth quarter three point shot at the buzzer for UCLA! Over the course of writing this book, I have developed a similar enthusiasm for local history. Historical author Ralph Pearce of the California Room at the San Jose King Library has spent countless hours supporting the publication of this book. His extensive research about Schurra's Candy was especially helpful in writing the Schurra's Candy historical vignette. Both Marilee Taylor and Susan Majeski volunteered time from their busy schedules to read and edit this publication.

I would like to thank the people and institutions who work tirelessly to ensure that our local history is preserved for future generations. The California Room at the San Jose King Library, the History San José Research Library at Kelley Park, the Santa Clara University Archives and The Sourisseau Academy all provided me with invaluable guidance, information, and vintage photographs.

Leonard McKay volunteered to provide color commentary during our first "History Walk" on The Alameda on October 14, 2006. Unfortunately, Leonard was unable to participate because he had been hospitalized. He passed away three days later. I am very grateful for Leonard McKay's involvement with and contributions to The Alameda – The Beautiful Way, especially during the final weeks of his life.

I am also honored to have received Leonard's feedback. During one of our final visits, Leonard was reading through my manuscript and exclaimed, "I've been reviewing your wonderful book on The Alameda. It's outstandingly - very, very good." Once again, Leonard was being very, very generous.

- Shannon E. Clark

Table of Contents

SCENE ON THE ALAMEDA.

I. The History of The Alameda

THE
ALAMEDA

The Beautiful Way

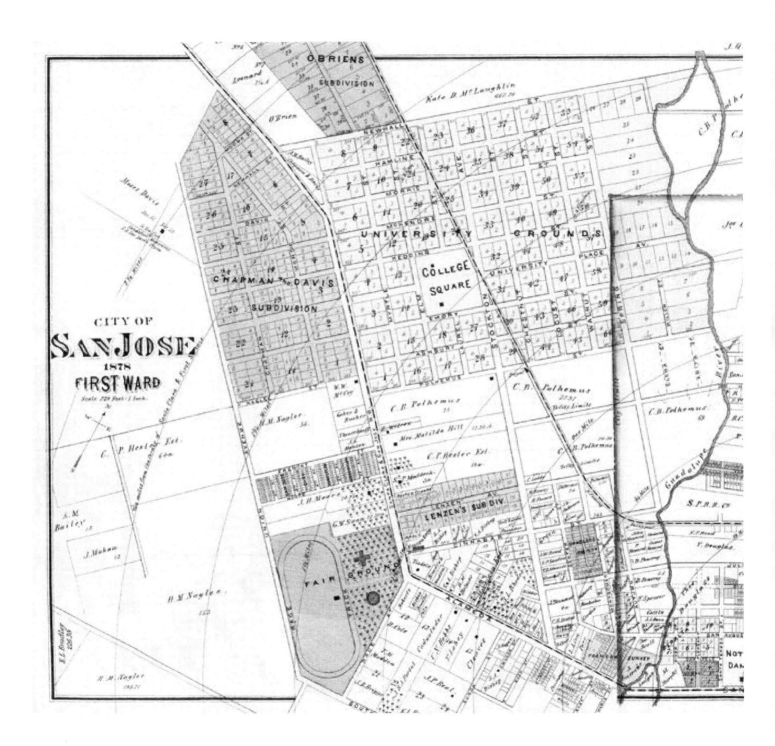

CITY OF
SAN JOSE
1878
FIRST WARD

Introduction

William A. Wulf

The Alameda might appear to the casual observer as just another fragment of the famous El Camino Real. In truth, The Alameda, the "road of a thousand wonders," is considered the "first true road" in California.[1] This avenue was renowned for its promenade of overarching willows planted by Father Magin de Catalá in 1799. The Alameda's history is replete with important firsts. California's first stagecoach line, the first interurban railroad on the West Coast, California's first co-educational college campus, the first music conservatory west of the Mississippi and the earliest cannery in Santa Clara County all had their origins on The Alameda. The Alameda lays claim to the landing of the world's first public exhibition of a manned high-air flight by virtue of John Montgomery's glider plane. California's earliest state fairs and cycling competitions occurred on The Alameda. If it happened, it probably happened first on The Alameda!

The stately willow trees on "the finest thoroughfare in the entire province of California" attracted the most successful early San Joseans.[2] They built their large, comfortable homes on this prestigious street. Even today, twenty-seven of those beautiful mansions survive as testimony to this desirable address.

Over the years, colorful figures have graced The Alameda with their stories and triumphs. Father Catalá, founder of this road, has been considered for sainthood. A. L. Rhodes, one of the first five settlers on The Alameda, rescued its residents from opportunistic land grabbers. At the turn of the century, John Montgomery was developing his theories of aerodynamics at the University of Santa Clara—advancing the field of aeronautics. Each of these great men has contributed to the varied history of The Alameda.

The Alameda played a crucial role in the development of San Jose and of California. California's early history revolved around this road—the link between the earliest civil settlement and the eighth Mission. The Alameda would always mark important beginnings and prosperous futures. As "one of the state's busiest boulevards," the street initially provided an avenue of trade and communication between the Santa Clara Mission and the early Pueblo de San Jose.[3] The Alameda has always paved the way towards prosperity and progress. With its numerous advances in transportation, The Alameda helped the local economy recover when the state capital was moved from San Jose to Vallejo. The Alameda spawned some of the earliest industries in the Santa Clara Valley and attracted some of the most successful innovators of San Jose.

The story of The Alameda presents the history of Santa Clara Valley through a unique perspective. Now, a seemingly forgotten storybook, the history of The Alameda has faded along with the original willow trees. This short history attempts to recapture the stories and myths of The Alameda so they are not lost to people, businesses, and organizations that call The Alameda home. The Alameda, with its roots first planted two centuries ago by Father Catalá, is reemerging as an important and unique place in the heart of Silicon Valley.

Origins of The Alameda

The Pueblo of San Jose was established on November 29, 1777, by Governor Felipe de Neve. The governor chose five civilians and nine soldiers from garrisons in Monterey and San Francisco to move to San Jose with their families. Just ten months before, Father Tomas de la Pena blessed the Mission Santa Clara as the eighth mission in California. The mission always had close ties to the Pueblo, but Father Magin de Catalá wanted to further bridge their three-mile gap. Catalá used The Alameda as this link.

Developments along The Alameda began around 1795 using the labor of neophytes. Young Indians were the first converts at the mission. For local Ohlone Indians, 1795

signified an increase in their dependency on the mission, as the number of adult converts increased dramatically. This new abundance of labor and the need for greater food production inspired Father Catalá to increase the flow of water between the Guadalupe River and the mission fields. Catalá first constructed *zanjas*, or irrigation ditches, in an effort to increase crop production. Father Catalá feared the possibility of rebellion if the Indians were not fed adequately, so increased irrigation capability was imperative.[1]

Each *zanja* was three *varas* wide (eight feet), and one and one-half *varas* deep (four feet).[2] Each was wide enough to accommodate Indian fishing boats from the Guadalupe River. The water from this river, which was so critical to the ongoing viability of the mission, found its way down both sides of The Alameda. Directed by land gradients for proper water flow, the *zanjas* passed the pear orchard and intersected Mission Creek (see map).[3] Mission Creek fed a *pozo*, or pond, near the Mission. With the passing of time, a lower water table caused both Mission Creek and the *zanjas* to dry up. The *zanjas* were filled and covered, but The

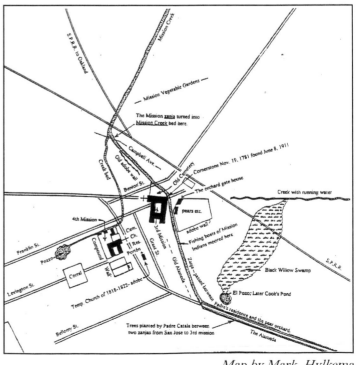

Map by Mark Hylkema

Alameda retains the distinctive and somewhat abrupt bend in the road corresponding to the layout of the original *zanjas*.

In 1799, two hundred neophytes lined The Alameda with willow saplings from the Guadalupe River. The neophytes also obtained some of the plantings from Cook's Pond, once located near New Maple Street in Santa Clara, east of The Alameda.[4] Water from the *zanjas* enabled the willow saplings to thrive. In the following years, neophytes tended the saplings to prevent wild cattle from knocking them down.[5]

Padre Jose Viader, Catalá's assistant, directed the transplanting of willows. Chief Marcello, a legendary 250-pound, six-foot-two descendant of the "royal Yumans of the valley of the Colorado River," oversaw the improvements along The Alameda. He is said to have lived a century and a quarter. Marcello was reportedly "the last of his race" and the "most famous of all the Mission Indians." Later in his life, Chief Marcello pointed out the exact course of the almost forgotten *zanjas* that were so familiar to him as a young man.[6]

Father Catalá had many reasons for creating "The Beautiful Way." The name of the road provides one reason why it was built. In Spanish, "Alameda" translates as "poplar grove," "shady walk," "wood," and "public walk."[8] Father Catalá had the San Jose settlers in mind when he built it. The Alameda provided the public with a pleasant stroll from the Pueblo de San Jose to the mission. With this attractive boulevard, Father Catalá hoped to "get backsliding settlers away from bear and bull fights and to mass on Sundays."[9]

Catalá coupled his motive of nurturing the spiritual health of the settlers with an apology for criticizing their un-Christian ways of life. The padres frequently condemned the settlers' negative influence on the mission Indians. The mission fathers harshly criticized the moral standards of the early settlers. The Alameda served as a conciliatory peace offering. Catalá hoped to rectify the wayward lifestyle of the settlers and to encourage them to turn to the church with this new and improved "public walk."[10]

This "shady walk" had a long-term,

Bea Lichtenstein

Cook's Pond

Major John A. Cook came to San Jose while representing San Diego County in the California Legislature when San Jose was the state capital. John Cook settled in Santa Clara and married Jane Fulkerson. They built a home just off The Alameda in the summer of 1853 on Deep Springs Lake, which later became known as Cook's Pond. This served as a recreational park through the years. In 1858, the first class to graduate from the male department of the University of the Pacific received its diplomas at Cook's Pond. Events that took place there include the Santa Clara College graduation ceremonies and the 1876 celebration of the nation's centennial.[7]

This early photo of Mission Santa Clara may have been the first photo taken in California. Note that the columns were painted, along with the rest of the facade.

practical function. In addition to encouraging Church attendance, the trees offered villagers protection from stray long-horned cattle along The Alameda.[11] In 1798, 3,000 head of cattle roamed the plains of Mission Santa Clara. By 1828, there were 14,500 head of cattle.[12] Attacks by long horned cattle were infrequent, yet widely feared. Around 1864, chains were strung along the willow trees to mitigate this threat.[13]

Improvements along The Alameda aided in establishing a "mission-pueblo contract."[14] The tree-lined street helped to resolve boundary disputes between the Mission Santa Clara and the pueblo villagers. In describing the boundary dispute, San Jose historian Fredrick H. Hall explains, "Although not as threatening in its aspect as the dispute on the northwest boundary between the United States and British America," the dispute was "not less warlike in words," and "sent forth principally in epistolary form."[15]

The land conflict emerged in 1797, when settlers tried to expand into land that was reserved for the neophytes.[16] Mission fathers complained that the pueblo settlers were a bad influence on their mission Indians and wanted the pueblo settlers to keep their distance.[17]

However, the missionaries and the pueblo settlers encroached upon each other's land. Mission livestock were corralled on the pueblo side of the Guadalupe River. Even though numerous boundary markers lay further west than the Guadalupe River, the Viceroy decreed that the Guadalupe River was the official mission/pueblo boundary on September 1, 1800.[18] As part of the compromise, the newly established road helped assuage the pueblo settlers' feelings of resentment.

The Alameda's most important purpose was to facilitate travel between the mission and the pueblo. Travelers encountered great difficulty traversing this area because the San Jose area was a marshland. Captain George Vancouver, the first Englishman to come to California, found it very difficult to travel between Mission Santa Clara and the Pueblo of San Jose. In 1792, he complained:

We advanced a few miles in an open clear meadow, and arrived in a low swampy country; through which our progress was very slow, the horses being nearly knee deep in mud and water for about six miles. The badness of our road rendered this part of our journey somewhat unpleasant.[19]

During winters before The Alameda was constructed, one had to make a circuitous six mile trek to the west in order to travel between the mission and the pueblo.[20] To an extent, The Alameda helped alleviate this problem. Chester Smith Lyman fondly recalls using the road in the middle of the 19th-century; "Being disappointed about a horse I footed it back to the Pueblo in season for breakfast at Capt. Webrs. The walk between the two places beneath the

California Room

This is possibly the earliest picture taken of The Alameda. It was taken in the late 1850s or early 1860s. It echoes the time when San Jose was a Mexican pueblo.

overarching rows of willows is delightful." The Alameda not only strengthened the relationship between the mission and the pueblo, but also provided a scenic and direct route for travelers visiting San Jose.

Willows

L ocal historians have disagreed about the actual number of rows of trees that Father Catalá and Marcello planted along "The Way of the Willows." Memory of the true willow arrangement may have disappeared with Chief Marcello's death in 1875. The controversy has raged on among historians for more than a century. The willows present a classic example of the loss of definitive historical truth relating to The Alameda. Oral tradition obscures the hard facts about the small community here. We may never know exactly what The Alameda looked like in 1799. However, there are still vestiges of the past that point toward a definitive truth.

Two Rows

In 1848, surveyors reported two rows of trees that were at least 40 years old.[1] In 1917, Rev. J. M O'Sullivan from the University of Santa Clara stated emphatically, "There were two rows of trees on the old Alameda road, and only two." He wrote, "In the course of time and mainly after the American occupation a third row of trees were planted which has given rise to the false tradition of three original rows. The third row were [sic] of wild willows (Pollard) interspersed with some poplars or sycamores. If three rows were planted west, middle, and east, the trees of the west line either died from neglect or were removed at an early date."[2] An early visitor to The Alameda gives credence to this argument. In 1847, Chester Smith Lyman boasted, "Our road from the mission to the pueblo was a beautiful one finely shaded by two rows of a species of willow."[3] In 1855, Rev. John Sessions, visiting from New York, wrote in his diary, "We went for three miles through the most delightful drive I ever saw…and there were two rows of old willows on the sides all the way."[4] However, there are two readings here—either that there were two rows total, or two rows shaded one lane, and additional rows of trees framed adjacent lanes.

Three Rows

Respected San Jose historians, such as Clyde Arbuckle, H. S. Foote, and William Ingraham Kip suggest that there were three original rows of willows. In *Early Days of My Episcopate*, published 1954, Kip states

Santa Clara University Archives

This photo, "The Ghost on The Alameda," was taken between 1868 and 1887, as indicated by the horsecar railroad tracks to the right.

This photo was taken by Andrew P. Hill from the present Race Street intersection, looking toward Santa Clara. The third row of trees on the left form the boundary of the Agricultural Park, with the Agricultural Park entrance in the foreground. To the far right is the Fredericksburg Resort.

that the willows "were planted by the old priests, in the days of their rule, and stand in three rows, one on one side, and two on the other where the footpath ran."[5] When work began on the first electric streetcar in 1887, three rows ran along The Alameda. Pictures from that time show three rows. Many sources recall hundreds of willows "still standing in the center line" in 1886.[6] One can conclude that there were at least three rows of willows at one point in time.

Sketch by Ralph Rambo

Carretas were the first vehicles of transportation in early California.

Four Rows

However, it is possible that Catalá originally planted a fourth row that disappeared before cameras began capturing The Alameda. The most extensive collection of research about the willow trees is that of Father Spearman, found in the Santa Clara University Archives.

Spearman explains that the "western central row" was removed to allow more passing space for carretas.[7] In 1934, a plaque was dedicated to the three last willows. At the plaquing ceremony, the Franciscan monk, Morris Ray, discussed the fourth row in his speech commemorating the three last willows. He said that the willows were thinned by removing the west middle row, with two rows

Note that the horsecar line coming from Santa Clara does not appear to run between two rows 8 to 10 feet apart on the east side, as Morris Ray stated, and there is a second lane on the left.

History San José

Looking towards San Jose in the 1870's. Note the recently planted trees in the middle row. *History San José*

on the east side 8-10 feet apart. The horsecar line later ran between the rows during the mid-19th-century. "A double lane separated the west row from these two east rows so that the quaint carretas with their horn-yoked oxen could pass," he explained.[8]

Spearman concluded that the remaining rows formed one narrow lane on the east side and a wide lane on the west. This gap itself suggests an original fourth row. Spearman cited a description of four rows given by Mrs.

P. J. Graham, who was married in the Mission Church in 1869, and the boyhood recollections of Mr. Joseph Scanlane, who was born in Santa Clara in 1873.[9]

Early removal of trees on The Alameda. *Santa Clara University Archives*

Best Explanation

There may be a plausible explanation to reconcile disagreement over the number of rows of willows on The Alameda. Simply put, The Alameda is three miles long and there may have been different numbers of rows planted in different sections of the street. The plantings were subject to the path of the *zanjas*. The area available for planting may have varied from place to place.

Removal of the trees was documented throughout the 19th century. Early settlers cut the willows for lumber when lumber was scarce in San Jose. In February 1833, Governor Figueroa issued a decree prohibiting the cutting of trees along The Alameda.[10] In 1847, the trunks of Alameda trees were used to fortify the gates of Mission Santa Clara during the Battle of Santa Clara—the only Northern California skirmish during the Bear Flag Rebellion.[11] These trees probably occupied the west end of The Alameda, near the Mission.

The historical account of the number of rows of trees depends where and when this historic street is viewed. Multiple accounts of the number of rows could be correct. Perhaps there were four rows in some places, and three rows in others. Still, the historical record is unclear. What we do know is that over time, all of the grand willows have vanished.

Type of Willow

Like the number of rows, the species of willow tree lining The Alameda is also a subject of dispute. Almost all historians state that Father Catalá shaded the road with red or black willows. One exception was in 1948, when Theron G. Cady claimed that "Gatala" planted over 16,000 Pollard willows.[12] It is possible that Pollard willows were present on The Alameda at some point in history, but the Pollard is a European species of willow. Other than this account, historians consistently describe the trees as either red or black willows. For example, Arbuckle states that the willows were red, while Spearman claims that they were black. Both species were probably present, since the Salix laevigata (Red Willow) and Salix goodingii (Goodings Black Willow) are both native to California. In fact, the Red Willow and Goodings Black Willow are so similar that one could have been easily mistaken for the other.

Photos suggest that the primary type of willow trees originally planted along The Alameda were Goodings Black Willows. The willow trees on The Alameda were massive. Some appear to be at least 45 feet tall, and the Goodings Black Willow can grow to twice the height of the Red Willow.

	Goodings Black Willow	Red Willow
Height	Under 30 meters (about 90 feet)	Under 15 meters (about 45 feet)
Leaf Texture	Finely cerrate (has teeth around edges), shiny surface, under-side of leaf hairy only when young	Finely cerrate, shinier surface, fine hairs on under-side of leaf
Leaf Shape	Long lancillate (generally narrower leaves)	Ranges from long lancillate to widely elliptic
Leaf Length	130 mm long	67-150 mm long
Twig Coloration	Yellowish	Red to yellowbrown
Location	Grows in marshes, river-banks, and meadows in California	

Father Magin de Catalá

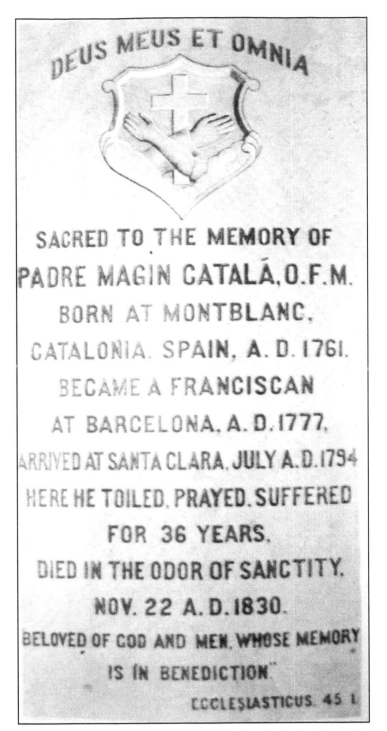

Father Magin de Catalá's signiture, from *The Holy Man of Santa Clara* by Fr. Zephyrin Englehardt

Father Magin de Catalá was a legendary character. Father Catalá was born on January 31, 1761 along with a twin brother in Tarragona, Spain.[1] He left Catalonia and arrived at the Santa Clara Mission in 1794. Living an austere life, Father Catalá abstained from wine during the thirty-six years he served as a priest.[2] He refused to eat until noon and abstained from meat, eggs and fish. He reputedly made all missionary trips within the valley barefoot.[3]

Father Catalá served as a charismatic leader and was acclaimed as a prophet. He foresaw events such as San Jose's epidemic of 1850 and the 1906 earthquake. He slept on an adobe brick pillow the size of a chair that was reputed to provide him with visions. In *The Holy Man of Santa Clara*, Encarnación Soto recalls one of Catalá's prophesies of an accidental death on The Alameda:

> Encarnacion Soto declared that she was present on one St. John's feast, when horse races were held as was usual on this day. Before leaving Santa Clara Fr. Magin warned the young men, and said, 'Do not hurry; be careful, for an accident is going to happen.' While racing, one of the young men, Juan Mesa, fell from his horse and was killed near the bridge of San Jose.[4]

In addition to prophetic powers, Catalá is said to have performed miracles. One time, Catalá saved fields and orchards of Santa Clara from locusts. In another account, he made water appear beneath a rock for the benefit of thirsty

Catalá's Gravestone   *Fr. Zephyrin Englehardt*

Indians, and then disappear. His greatest miracle on The Alameda took place in 1824 when he reportedly rescued the mission and pueblo crops. A drought that year caused 5,000 sheep to perish. During mass in April, Father Catalá prayed for rain and led a procession of neophytes with lighted candles down The Alameda. Secundino Robles recounts walking halfway to the pueblo then back, explaining:

When the praying multitude had reached the last station of the Way of the Cross erected along the Alameda, a black cloud was seen far away in the mountains to the west. It grew larger and wider and approached rapidly…rain began to fall in torrents and it was accompanied by a heavy wind. We boys wondered greatly that the candles which we bore were not extinguished by the wind, but kept on burning. Much rain fell for seven or eight days…I remember this well, for I was about fourteen years old, and was one of the boys that carried candles.[5]

It is also said that Father Catalá frightened a "whole legion of devils" away by reciting prayers as he walked down The Alameda. Father Zephyrin Englehardt noted,

[T]hat the Alameda especially must have annoyed the powers of darkness, may be well understood from the fact that the fourteen Stations of the Cross lined the road.[6]

Father Magin de Catalá's pillow, filled with flecks of steel, ash, and gold, is on display in the California Room at the San Jose City Library.

Corpus Christi Altares de Enramada

When Reverend Henry Woods, S. J. walked along The Alameda in 1878, he noted recessed spaces at intervals planned for the Corpus Christi procession enramadas. The altars were lined with exquisitely embroidered shawls imported from China and were framed over by willow branches. The procession of the Blessed Sacrament would stop at each station while the priest rested the Sacred Host on the altar table during a hymn. Encarnación Pinedo also told the story of the "Way of the Cross." On Good Friday, three men dressed in white linen vestments would carry a "very heavy crucifix" along The Alameda, stopping at the stations along the way.[7]

Santa Clara University Archives
There are no known, accurate pictures of Father Catalá, but this is a depiction of him preaching to the Indians of Santa Clara.

Transportation

San Jose became California's capital in 1849. Lack of facilities, flooding and poor organization hindered this "Legislature of a Thousand Drinks." When the state capital was moved to Vallejo in 1853, the San Jose economy was devastated. With numerous innovative advances in transportation, The Alameda assisted San Jose's economic recovery over the following decade.

The Alameda's first transportation related enterprise was the stagecoach. John Whisman opened the first stagecoach line in California.[1] His stage began commuting daily between San Francisco and San Jose in September, 1849, and charged a $35, one-way fare. The next year, Messrs. Ackley and Morrison (or Maurison) opened a competing line. Whisman reduced the fare to $10, but the price decrease led him to sell the line to Warren F. Hall and Jared B. Crandall in 1850.[2] In 1854, the fare was reduced to two dollars.[3] In 1856, The Crandall Brothers established an omnibus line on The Alameda. This French omnibus was similar to a stagecoach, with windows on either side, but passengers entered through the back. The line ran on The Alameda from the Cameron House in Santa Clara to the Auzerias House in San Jose. William Fitts, a pioneer from Maine, came to San Jose in 1850. He drove the omnibus and eventually became the first driver of The Alameda horsecar railroad.

The transportation business was highly competitive along The Alameda because it was such a well-traveled road. In 1862, Hiram Shartzer began the Alameda Turnpike Company, which operated one of the early toll roads of California. He built the tollgate at what is now West Julian Street (formerly

William A. Wulf

"Billy" Fitts started his own omnibus line two years after the Crandall Brothers, which ran until the San Jose & Santa Clara Horse Railroad put him out of business in 1868. Fitts' two mustangs were faster than the horse-car, but the 25-cent omnibus struggled to compete with the 10-cent horsecar. He is credited as the last of the pre-rail stage drivers and the first of the horse car drivers on The Alameda. Fitts became superintendent of horsecar line, driving until its electrification. He then went to work for the San Jose Water Company.

Cinnabar Street) and charged 10 cents for single buggies, 25 cents for teams, and $1 for stages.[4] During this time, advances in transportation like California's first stagecoach line and toll road helped the economy surrounding The Alameda.

An even more ambitious project was the building of the railroad connecting San Francisco and San Jose, which also aided in San Jose's economic recovery. Californians began dreaming of this railroad as early as 1851, when William J. Lewis created its rough sketch. That year, the Pacific and Atlantic Railroad Company was incorporated by the most prominent San Joseans, including vice president James Alexander Forbes (For more information about Forbes, see page 26). Construction

was ready to begin when the financial panic of 1854–1855 hit. This first movement towards building the railroad failed because it ran out of support and funding. In 1860, the railroad company tried to reorganize as The San Francisco and San Jose Railroad and secured permission from the state to hold a $900,000 stock subscription election. Opposition from a San Francisco newspaper helped this movement to fail as well.

Santa Clara County agreed to fund the railroad with $200,000 worth of bonds. On August 18, 1860, C. T. Ryland formed the next railroad company. Dr. Davis Divine, Charles B. Polhemus, Peter Donahue, and Henry M. Newhall backed the enterprise. This company encountered obstacles, but ultimately succeeded.

The Alameda bordered the 1939-acre Stockton Ranch, which was on the planned path of the proposed railroad. The project was about to collapse until Charles B. Polhemus, Peter Donahue, and Henry M. Newhall bought the ranch from Commodore Stockton for $110,000.[5] Also, to fund the railroad, they sold $285,000 worth of private subscriptions. Only $100,000 worth of subscriptions were actually paid. Polhemus, Donahue, and Newhall bought the stock, enabling the railroad to begin construction in May 1861. The San Francisco and San Jose Railroad first reached its terminus on San Pedro Street

Society of California Pioneers

Photo of Hiram Shartzer's tollgate in the 1860's. The toll road began at the edge of the City of San Jose and ended in Santa Clara. Clyde Arbuckle states that the tollgate was at Julian Street. People frequently took Stockton Avenue to avoid the toll, then merged onto The Alameda via Cinnabar Street (West Julian Street and Cinnabar Street used to connect as one street called Cinnabar Street).

on January 16, 1864 with a 36-gun salute. The California Guard fired its cannon as crowds cheered the locomotive into the station. J. J. Owen of the *San Jose Mercury* reported,

> It should be a source of pride and gratitude to every true American citizen that while we, as a nation, are passing through the fiery surges of a terrible war, we can with one hand build railroads and telegraphs, establish schools for the promotion of science, and wrest from the willing soil its rich treasures and bounteous harvests, while with the other hand we can throttle the hounds that are tearing at the vitals of constitutional liberty. The Pacific railroad is no longer an idle dream slumbering in the brain of the statesmen. It has a tangible shape and a visible reality. We hail the consummation of this enterprise as one of the proudest achievements of our state.[6]

This railroad was an invaluable asset to San Jose and it was made possible by some of the first residents and landowners on The Alameda.

The San Francisco and San Jose Railroad Company "opened a new era of prosperity" for San Jose.[7] Immediately, business improved in the area. Stages were receiving more business than ever because of the increase in population. The railroad brought new, thriving industries to The Alameda such as the Fredericksburg Brewery and helped old industries, like milling, find new markets. Real estate values skyrocketed. By 1867, a half-acre of commercial land was selling for a price as high as $18,000.[8] San Jose's economy, formerly ranching based, became an agricultural "nerve center" for California.[9]

Like most early developments in San Jose, early transportation developments on The Alameda were hindered by San Jose's rain and mud. During the winter, the stagecoach line was rerouted to Alviso due to mud (from Alviso, San Joseans would then take a steamship to San Francisco). The Alameda Turnpike Company struggled to function efficiently due

William A. Wulf

to the mud caused by the shade of the willow trees. After heavy winter rains, The Alameda was impassable. People were forced to take a six-mile detour to travel from Santa Clara to San Jose, despite Catalá's early efforts to prevent this. H.S. Foote claims, "four or five months in the year it was almost impassable for vehicles. Travelers passing between the town of Santa Clara and San Jose were compelled to seek the side of the road, and often to make a circuit of four or five miles…" In fact, there was so much mud that Santa Clara County had to open an alternative road parallel to The Alameda. This road was called Union Avenue, now Park Avenue.[10] However, Union Avenue was never as popular as the delightful shaded thoroughfare, The Alameda.[11] People preferred The Alameda even with its mud!

Since The Alameda Turnpike Company could not maintain the road, people begged Santa Clara County to buy The Alameda route back from Shartzer. In 1868, the County purchased The Alameda Turnpike Company franchise for $17,737.50.[12]

Samuel Addison Bishop initiated the next transportation advancement. Bishop moved to The Alameda in 1867. Though a 300-pound Indian fighter and Virginian, he had a weakness for attending operas.[13] In

15

1851, President Fillmore named him State Superintendent of Indian Affairs. Having arrived with $200,000 in his pocket, this determined entrepreneur invested in mining, lumber, transportation, real estate, and finance throughout his lifetime. He eventually became the vice president of the San Jose Savings Bank and is regarded as the father of the San Jose local transit system.

On March 24, 1868, a Legislative Act declared Bishop part of an association to run a year-round horse railroad along The Alameda. Bishop completed the San Jose and Santa Clara Railroad on the first of November of that year. As California's first inter-urban horsecar railroad, it could withstand the harsh winter rains better than any previous Alameda vehicle. The rails ran along the north center of The Alameda and swung to higher ground on the east side after hitting the bend at the Agricultural Park (the Race Street intersection). The railroad ended at Franklin and Main Street in Santa Clara. The trip from San Jose to Santa Clara took 45 minutes.

Mischief-makers made the work of the railroad conductors, like Billy Fitts, more difficult. A few creative citizens were inspired by the fact that the horsecar line skirted Cook's Pond. The legislature had to pass an ordinance forbidding duck-hunting from streetcars.[14] The horsecar was designed with a ladder on the side so people could sun themselves on the roof while traveling. Schoolboys enjoyed climbing to the roof and crowding on the back of the

Samuel A. Bishop

Sourisseau Academy

car. Their weight would cause the entire car to teeter. Horsecar delays were frequent. One obstreperous schoolboy wrestled the reins away from the conductor. The mischief maker told the conductor to take a passenger seat as he drove to Santa Clara. On the Fourth of July, people enjoyed throwing firecrackers beneath the cars to scare the horses. One horse, after a firework exploded, freed himself from the car and earned the reputation of being a "circus horse."[15]

In 1869, Bishop extended his line to Coyote Creek at 17th Street, making the route four and a half miles long. The horses were strained by this distance; consequently, Bishop obtained permission from the County Board of Supervisors in 1870 to test alternative means of propulsion including steam and pneumatic propelling power. In 1871, Bishop found a steam dummy and tested it along The Alameda. However, San Jose's governing board decided soon afterward that Bishop did not have the right to propel by steam, according to the restrictions of his franchise.[16]

Bishop's San Jose and Santa Clara Railroad merged with Jacob Rich's People's Horse Railroad in 1882. The two dreamed of creating the first electrified streetcar in California, but controversy over what type of streetcar should be built delayed this dream. One faction of San Jose wanted overhead power; the other did not. Cable car proponents pointed out the success of the San Francisco cable cars. Proponents of an electrified

This horsecar was The Alameda's competing line on Stockton Avenue. *William A. Wulf*

underground system believed that overhead lines were dangerous and unsightly. San Jose granted a franchise for the San Jose and Santa Clara Railroad to build a car with underground power in 1887, but the Town of Santa Clara did not.[17]

Frustrated, Bishop and Rich set out to find an electric railroad that would satisfy government officials. They traveled to Denver, Kansas City, Windsor, Canada and Baltimore, and finally found the Fisher System in Detroit. Frank E. Fisher of the Detroit Electric Works

was an ambitious 27-year-old who was working on a streetcar system in Highland Park. The Fisher System used a third, center rail for its electric power. Fisher proposed that the third rail could be buried below the ground in their line, satisfying the safety concerns of the Town of Santa Clara.[18]

In the 1880s, the decaying condition of the center line of willows on The Alameda began to endanger travelers. Their shade also made it difficult for the horse railroad to operate at dusk and in the rain. As a result, residents

William A. Wulf

Workers laying the rails for Bishop's Fisher Electric Railway in 1887.   *History San José*

petitioned the Board of Supervisors' office to remove the trees. W. O. Watson, the supervisor of the 4th District, approved their removal in July 1887.

It is said that the center row of willows was removed secretly at night for safety reasons. Spearman notes that the roots and stumps of the removed willow trees were hauled to fill in Cook's Pond, because the artesian wells had drained the pond dry. Later, the Pacific Manufacturing Company built its factory over this land fill.

On October 5, 1887, Bishop began converting his narrow-gauge steam line into the second electric streetcar in California. If not for government opposition and numerous construction delays, it could have been the first streetcar in California. San Diego's streetcar system began running only months before San Jose's. Cement shortages, labor strikes, and competing rail projects like the Southern

Pacific Railroad extended construction until March 16, 1888. Nonetheless, Bishop's line is considered the first *interurban* electric streetcar of the West.[19]

Dummy No. 5 was the first electric streetcar to traverse The Alameda. On its maiden run, the car carried 43 passengers from the Coyote Creek Bridge toward Santa Clara, but struck a protruding metal insulator cap 150 yards short of the Agricultural Park.[20] Mrs. Lida Mae Gillette fondly recalls, "We got almost to the Fredericksburg Brewery when the car stopped. We saw all kinds of sparks and flashes coming from the ground under the car, and we all had to walk back to town." Since it was built with underground rail, muddy streets and curious pedestrians caused frequent streetcar delays. Pedestrians were fascinated by the dazzling spectacle of a shorted circuit and frequently stuck metal objects or umbrellas into the power slots to see the sparks.[22]

Santa Clara University Archives

"Embarking on one of the handsome cars of the Electric Road we are whirled rapidly along the famous Alameda Avenue, with its leafy shade, past the homes of wealthy men, sheltered with giant trees and embowered in flowers, to a point where stirring life and bustling activity proclaimed the presence of some great enterprise. It is the Fredericksburg Brewery, the widest known and the most extensive establishment of its kind west of the Rocky Mountains."[21] The chimney of the Fredericksburg Brewery can be seen behind J. H. Henry's streetcars.

Loryea Brothers, Photographers.   Electric Railway.   San Jose, California.
THOMSON-HOUSTON SYSTEM.

William A. Wulf

The Alameda, looking east, in the 1890's. The building to the far right is labeled, "Bowling Alley."

James H. Henry solved the spark problem by purchasing the San Jose and Santa Clara Railroad for $229,000 in 1889. He transformed it into the first electric trolley of its kind in California, with overhead electric lines that were out of the reach of curious pedestrians.[21] When The Alameda was paved in 1912, the mud problem was eliminated. Shade at that point in time was provided mainly by sycamores and elms.

Postcard depicting The Alameda.

William A. Wulf

William A. Wulf

The streetcar barn on the corner of Lenzen Avenue and The Alameda ca. 1910. These old frame and sheet iron streetcar barns were abandoned in 1938.[23] The willow tree to the right of the S. J. & S.C Railroad Company building is characteristic of Catalá's willows on The Alameda.

Residential Development

Early Settlement

Before it became a bustling avenue, The Alameda bordered two land grants, El Potrero de Santa Clara to the north and Los Coches to the south. After the secularization of the missions, the Mexican government opened mission land to the public. El Potrero de Santa Clara (Saint Clare's Colt Pasture) and Los Coches (The Pigs) were originally owned by Mission Santa Clara. Governor Micheltorena emancipated a Native American named Roberto Balermino (or Valermino) on March 12, 1844 and granted him Rancho Los Coches. Roberto lived there for about a decade in a small adobe house. On January 1, 1847, Roberto sold his 2219.341 acres to Antonio Maria Suñol, the first postmaster and a well-educated settler of San Jose. Suñol was

Antonio Maria Suñol

California State Library

of Spanish descent, but served Napoleon until he jumped ship in Monterey and came to San Jose in 1818.[1] Much of his wealth came from the milling industry and his investment in the New Almaden Quicksilver mines. He was also an *alcalde*, or judge.[2] The small adobe, built by Roberto in 1839, is now located on Lincoln Avenue, with Sunol Street a block away.

Governor Micheltorena granted El Potrero de Santa Clara to James Alexander Forbes in 1844. Three years later, Commodore Robert F. Stockton negotiated the purchase of Forbes' land for $10,500.[3] This initiated an early Alameda controversy. Forbes claimed that El Potrero encompassed 6,000 acres. Stockton discovered, to his dismay, that the rancho only comprised of 1939.03 acres.[4]

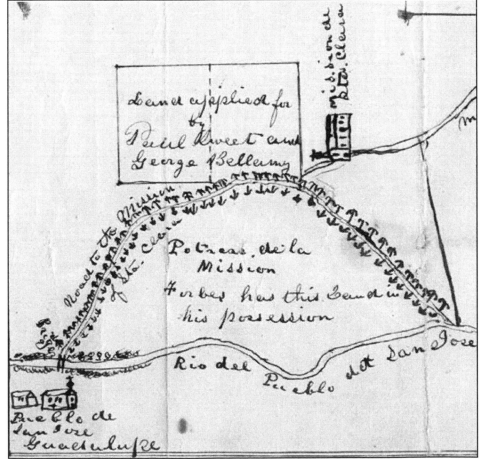

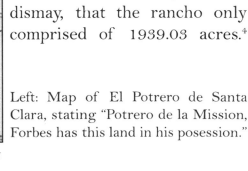

Left: Map of El Potrero de Santa Clara, stating "Potrero de la Mission, Forbes has this land in his posession."

History San José

James Alexander Forbes

William A. Wulf

Robert F. Stockton

History San José

The U.S. Land Commission and District Court verified this figure.[5] According to historian Frank L. Beach, Stockton's agent offered Forbes the money before the actual size of the acreage was known, and subsequently it was mutually agreed that the land should be surveyed. Ultimately, the acreage proved to be more than enough. Stockton designated a portion of this

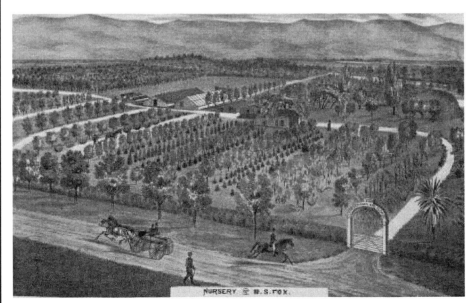

NURSERY @ B.S.FOX.

Thompson & West Historical Atlas

Stockton arrived in California in 1846 as the Commander of the Pacific Squadron during the war with Mexico. After serving as the military governor of California, he returned to the East Coast in 1847. He never revisited his land in California, but managed it from New Jersey. In the 1850s, he served as the Governor of New Jersey. In 1850, he ordered the Alameda Gardens to be mapped. In 1853, he sent a botanist, B.F. Fox, with a large stock of plants to establish a nursery. Along with asparagus and strawberries, this nursery housed the first hive of honeybees in California.[6]

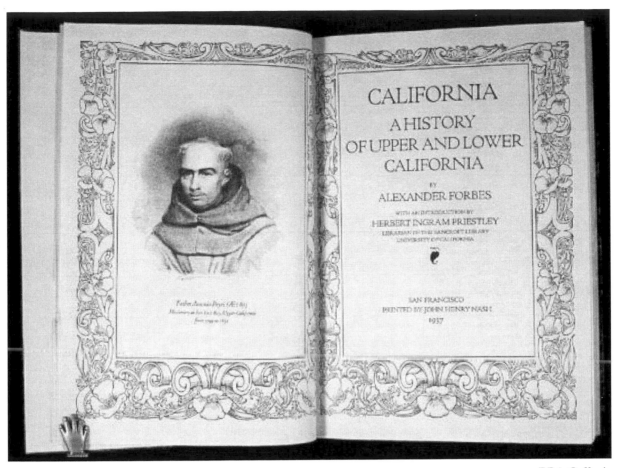

James Alexander Forbes may have written the first English history of California, published in London in 1839. Some argue that this "Alexander Forbes" was not James Alexander Forbes, but instead, the British Consul in Tepic, Mexico, Alexander Forbes. Alexander Forbes never visited California, but was in close contact with James Alexander Forbes, and was possibly his uncle.

land as the Alameda Gardens, one of San Jose's first subdivisions.

In Santa Clara Valley, the house-building industry was undeveloped and there was a scarcity of labor during the gold rush years. It is said that Stockton ordered 60 pre-fabricated houses to be transported from Philadelphia in 1849 for his subdivision. However, upon arriving in San Francisco the houses were destroyed by fire.[7] Subsequently, he ordered up to sixteen more homes from Massachusetts.[8] It was not uncommon for wealthy landowners to pick out pre-fabricated houses on the San Francisco wharfs. Stockton's houses were assembled by his agent, Mr. James F. Kennedy, one of the first sheriffs of Santa Clara County.[9] Prestigious residents of The Alameda including A. L. Rhodes, John H. Polhemus, Charles B. Polhemus, and D. M. Delmas owned these pre-fabricated houses. All of Stockton's houses were made from the same plans, except for one larger, more pretentious ranch house at the terminus of Spring Street, now within the area of the San Jose airport. Each house was two stories tall with a wide front porch extending the full length of the house. The stylish houses attracted wealthy pioneers from all over the county to The Alameda. However, the Alameda Gardens subdivision had limited success and much of it remained undeveloped.

Decades later, after advances in transportation made The Alameda more accessible, a new subdivision in this area was more successful—the College Park suburb.

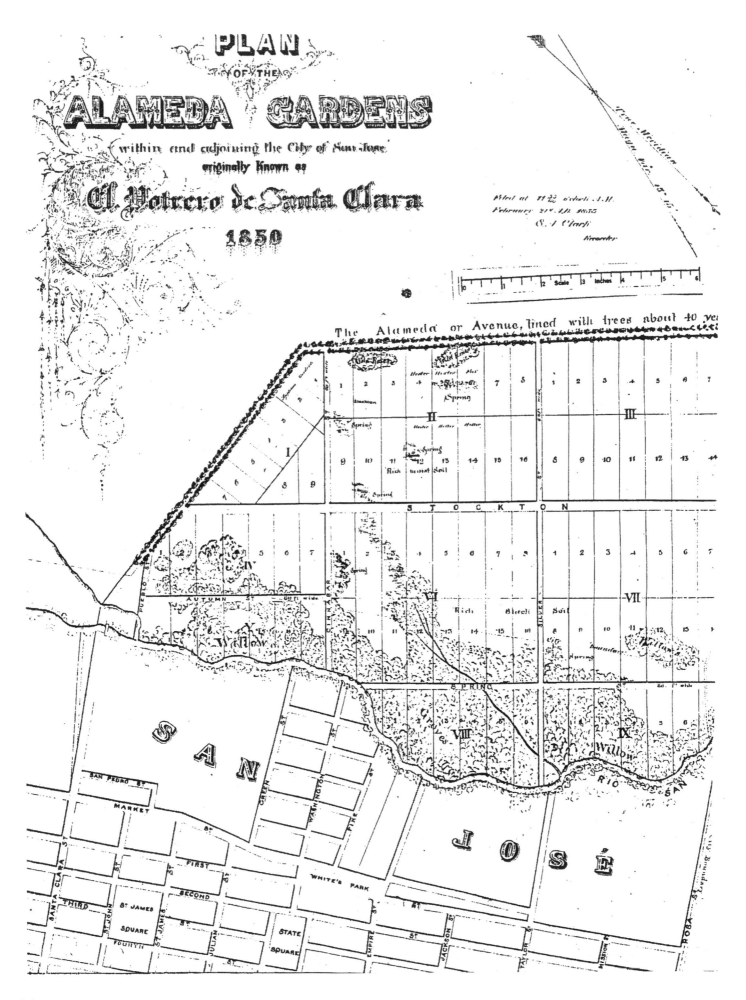

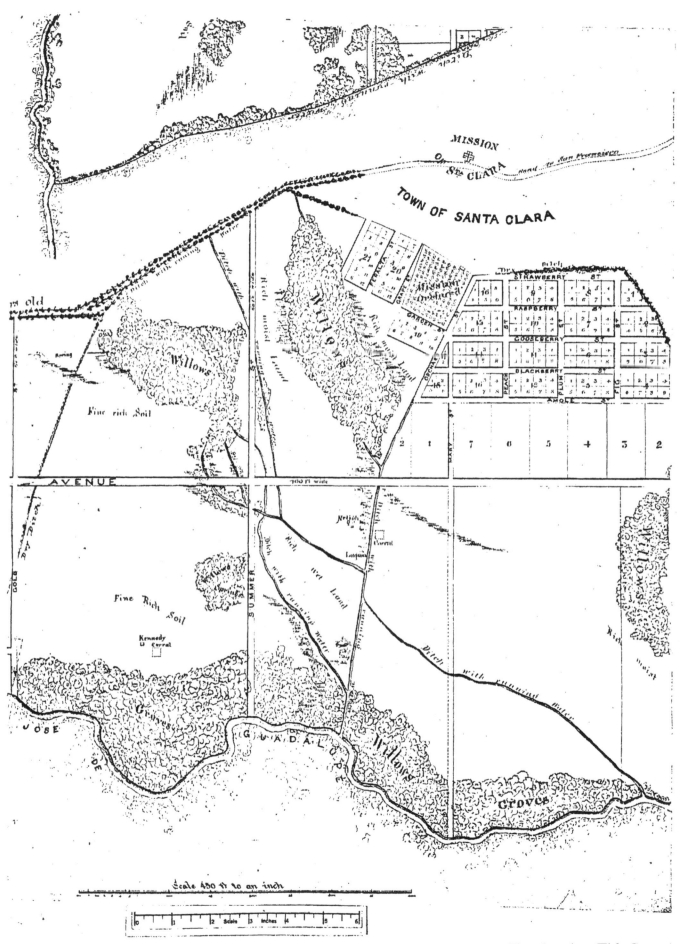

Scale 450 ft to an inch

25

James Alexander Forbes

(1805-1881)

James Alexander Forbes, the second owner of El Portero de Santa Clara, is a highly controversial early settler on The Alameda. Many accounts of him may be myth, with a definitive record of his life forever lost. Some believe that Forbes was a well-respected and talented businessman. Others view this man as an infamous mischief-maker.

Forbes was born to Marta Rodriguez and John Alonzo Forbes in Inverness, Scotland. After John Alonzo passed away in 1817, James Alexander was adopted by his uncle. One account states that he moved to Cadiz, Spain, to live with his uncle William Forbes and graduated from the College of Salamanca.

Another account suggests that Marta's brother, Francisco Rodriguez, brought James Alexander Forbes to Buenos Aires, Argentina. In Argentina, Rodriguez owned a shipping line that transported cattle and wheat to England. Rodriguez sent Forbes to the Jesuit College of Montevideo, Uruguay. In 1825, Montevideo became the epicenter of a war between Brazil and Argentina. Despite Rodriguez' economic ties to Argentina, Forbes sided with Brazil. Eighteen-year-old Forbes took one of Rodriguez' ships to combat. Forbes' cousin was killed. To prevent Forbes' execution, Rodriguez paid a large sum of money to Argentine officials and fled the country with Forbes to Conception, Chile. Rodriguez was killed in an earthquake there in 1828.

In 1829, Forbes set sail north, earning his passage until he abandoned ship at Yerba Buena (now San Francisco). The ambitious and amiable 26-year-old next arrived at Mission Santa Clara.

Padre Jose Viader immediately realized Forbes' business talents and

William A. Wulf

This is Forbes' mansion on Washington Street in Santa Clara, built in 1852. It stood there for 98 years, serving as the Notre Dame Convent for the majority of the time.

granted him the important position of majordomo—the chief clerk for the mission. Forbes was now in charge of the mission's financial records and property maintenance of Mission Santa Clara.

In 1834, Forbes married Ana Maria Galindo, the daughter of Juan Crisostomo Galindo. Some believe that Juan Crisostomo Galindo provided a generous dowry—the property known as El Potrero de Santa Clara. Governor Michaeltorena verified Forbes' ownership of the nine-square miles of land on February 22, 1844. James Alexander and Ana Maria had 12 children. The Forbes family occupied a quadrangle of the mission until he built a house on Washington Street, later home to the Notre Dame Convent.

Around 1841, Forbes became an agent for the British Hudson Bay Company. On December 7, 1842, Consul Eustace Barron at Tepic recommended Forbes as British Vice Consul of California, a position that he served until 1850.

At Mission Santa Clara, both Father Catalá and Father Viader helped James Alexander Forbes write the first history of California. California: a History of Upper and Lower California comprised of a compilation of Forbes' notes related to his journey in California. In this book he strongly advocated England's acquisition of California from Mexico by financial means. Historian Bill Wulf notes that the British consul of Mexico may have sent Forbes to investigate California on behalf of England.

Forbes' business venture, the New Almaden Quicksilver Mines, led to protracted ownership litigation in which Forbes incurred some $18,000 in lawyer's fees and court costs. Forbes was accused of forgery and antedating of documents. Either Forbes was truly a mischief-maker, or

this controversy tainted his reputation and gave rise to the false notion that he was a dishonest man.

Forbes hoped to provide his twelve children a Jesuit education and offered Jesuit fathers in Oregon $10,000 to start a school at Mission Santa Clara. When the Jesuit fathers arrived, Forbes graciously provided them with his rooms in the mission quadrangle to begin the school. According to a noted historian, Forbes then demanded $11,000 from the fathers to build a mansion for himself in Santa Clara. The Jesuit fathers wrote to the Vatican, which, in turn, appropriated the money. Some historians credit Forbes with "helping" found what is now Santa Clara University. However, the way that he received this credit appears somewhat self-serving.

Forbes' next business failure was his Los Gatos flourmill, which caused him to go bankrupt. As a solution to his economic woes, he helped found another school, Notre Dame. He sold his mansion to the sisters of Notre Dame for $8,000 in 1864 and eventually moved to Oakland with his wife. Later, the Sisters of Notre Dame discovered that the mansion had a lien of $20,000, which they were forced to pay, according to Bill Wulf. Whether Forbes' influence in the Santa Clara Valley was positive or negative is a question debated by historians. In any event, Forbes left his mark on the local economy, the mission, and The Alameda where he first settled.

Sources:

William A. Wulf, Los Gatos Historian.

Spearman Papers, Santa Clara University Archives.

Frank L. Beach, "James Alexander Forbes 1804–1881: British Vice Consul in California, 1842–1856," (Masters thesis presented to the Faculty of the Department of History, University of San Francisco, Jan. 1957).

Notable Residences on The Alameda

Bishop's horsecar was partly responsible for making The Alameda a prestigious address in the 1800's. The most desirable places to live in San Jose during the early days included The Alameda, North First Street, and Naglee Park near 10th street, because these streets were the first to have public transportation. Parking was a problem even back then. The wealthiest families had the luxury of taking the horsecar into town and conveniently left their horses and buggies at home. **In the following pages, each number on the map below corresponds to the residential history of that location.**

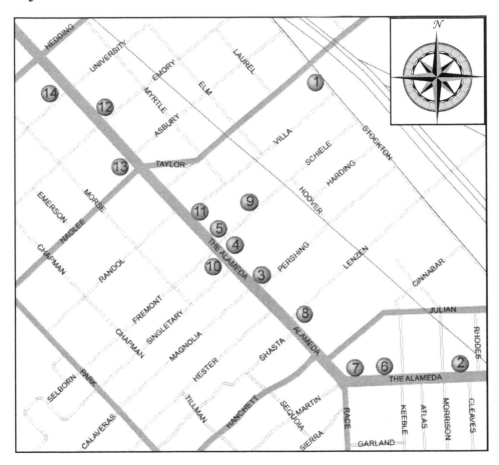

① The Polhemus Brothers

Charles Bispham Polhemus and Henry M. Newhall purchased 1,939 acres of the Stockton ranch, which included the undeveloped portion of Alameda Gardens This left Commodore Stockton 110 acres. As discussed previously, Polhemus and Newhall purchased the ranch in order to rescue the San Francisco-San Jose railroad enterprise from collapsing. Newhall divided his land into parcels and sold them by 1876, while Charles B. Polhemus and his descendants owned land in the area until after World War II.

At age 17, Charles Bispham Polhemus, born in New Jersey, joined his older brother John Hart Polhemus in South America. Polhemus lived in Valparaiso (Chile), Guayaquil (Ecuador), Lima and Paita (Peru). In Paita, he was the U.S. Consul for four years. After moving to San Francisco in 1851, Charles Polhemus was consul for Chile and Peru between 1850 and 1860 and was involved with importing and exporting for twenty years.[10] In 1858, he moved his family to San Mateo County after acquiring a large tract of land there, which now comprises the City of San Mateo. In

Charles Bispham Polhemus

Sourisseau Academy

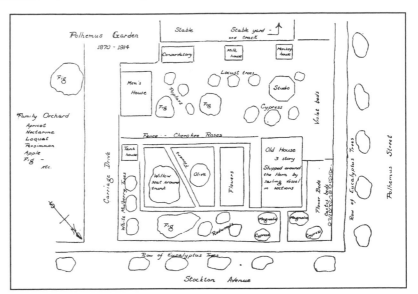

Vignettess of the Gardens of San Jose de Guadalupe

The "old house" shown on this map was built in hardwood sections in Massachusetts. The Charles B. Polhemus family named this house "Pendennis," and Charles' niece Ellen (Nellie) designed the garden. This house burned to the ground in 1914.

1869, Charles B. Polhemus moved to Laurel Wood, a ranch outside of Santa Clara. By the mid 1870s, after selling Laurel Wood to Peter Donahue, Polhemus moved his family to one of the Stockton prefabricated houses located at the southwest corner of Stockton and Taylor Streets. He named this estate "Pendennis."[11]

By 1870, John H. Polhemus moved into a house on The Alameda that he called the "Maple Hut." John was the agent for the sale of Stockton Rancho lands belonging to his brother Charles. "Maple Hut," which is said to have also been one of the Stockton prefabricated houses, burned down not long after the family located there. John and his family were living in a house at the northeast corner of Julian Street and Stockton Avenue called "The Cottage" at the time of his death in 1880.

The Polhemus family replaced "Pendennis" in 1919 with a wooden house of Dutch Colonial architecture. After World War II it was moved from the corner of Taylor Street and Stockton Avenue to the northwest corner of the Bellarmine campus. The house is now called Berchman Hall.[12]

Photo by Rex Kuehner

② Judge A. L. Rhodes

The only houses on The Alameda in 1862 were those of Judge A. L. Rhodes, J. R. Johnson, Judge Craven P. Hester, John Morse, and "Appleton."[13] Rhodes captained a wagon train to California and in 1858 moved into one of Commodore Stockton's pre-fabricated houses planned for his Alameda Gardens

Sourisseau Academy

Before Rhodes lived in this house, Baron von Bendeleben von Ackermann lived there. This Saxon noble was exiled during the revolution of 1848.[16]

subdivision.[14] This two-story home at 919 The Alameda survived until 1927, when it was demolished.[15]

In the 19th and early 20th centuries, The Alameda was the most fashionable address for prominent San Jose attornies. Gregory B. McCandless notes that in 1915 only doctors and lawyers lived north of Magnolia on The Alameda. He also calculated that in 1915, 74% of all occupations of Alameda residents were managerial and professional, and 22% of all directory listings on The Alameda were doctors and lawyers.[17]

Judge A. L. Rhodes played a part in a controversy on The Alameda that arose in 1870. The Alameda was 150 feet wide in the mid 19th century, but a rumor spread that the public road overlapped free land. In the middle of the night, squatters claimed bits of The Alameda by building makeshift wooden fences in front of actual properties, blocking some Alameda residences from the road. The squatter problem was resolved when the federal government confirmed that the land belonged to the County of Santa Clara and the City of San Jose. Judge Rhodes secured state and national legislation in 1871, fixing the width of the road at 115 feet. The extra land was granted to the owners of the properties along The Alameda and was clearly marked by stakes in 1872.

Rhodes had a great appreciation for the willows along The Alameda. He signed a less-popular petition against the removal of the center row of trees in 1887. The petition recommended that Bishop "locate Said tracks in Such a way that Said Center row of trees may not be disturbed."[18]

③ Judge Craven P. Hester

Craven P. Hester, district attorney for San Jose and later judge of the Third Judicial District, owned 19 acres on the east side of The Alameda between Pershing and Schiele Avenues. In 1850, Judge Hester, his wife, and four children moved into a small adobe house in the center of town. One daughter, Sallie P. Hester, kept a diary between 1850 and 1871.

Matthias Hester

Matthias Hester, the father of Judge Craven P. Hester, was a German immigrant. He enjoyed telling his 11 children the tale of the time when Indians attacked the team and wagon that he was driving in Kentucky in 1790. The Indians apparently shot, speared, tomahawked and scalped twenty-one year old Matthias, but he lived to tell his grandchildren about it. "Well, I was riding one of the lead horses when the Indians attacked the wagons. Two of them fired from ambush and a ball grazed my scalp. I took off on foot, the two Indians right behind me. I ran and ran. I could hear them gaining on me when I stumbled and fell in a creek bed. On of them swung his tomahawk, and I thought I was a goner."[19]

RES. *of the late* HON. C. P. HESTER, *San Jose, California.*

Residence of C. P. Hester. The mischievous students of the University of the Pacific were known for their pranks. Some liked to climb onto the roofs of the Alameda horsecar and grab onto overhanging willow branches.[20]

On March 30, 1852 she notes, "My father has bought property on the Alameda Road and we expect to move out soon to the place where we are going to build. We have rented the Stockton House which came round the horn. The Alameda is an Avenue of Willows." And in May, "We have moved out on the road. We like it much better than in town."

In July of 1852, the Hester family moved into the big house built on The Alameda. Sallie describes, "The place is blooming with wild roses so I named it "Wild Rose Farm."" In 1857, Judge Hester won many prizes for his horticultural exhibits.

Hester is noted for helping to organize the Methodist Church in San Jose and was a prominent trustee of the University of the Pacific. In the *History of the University of the Pacific*, Rockwell D. Hunt notes that "legal advice of such men of capacity and integrity as Judge Hester…cannot be minimized."

As one of the first residents of The Alameda, Hester was a well-respected attorney and judge. The Hester Theater (now the Towne Theater), Hester Avenue, the Hester District, Hester School, the Hester Market and Hester Pharmacy (both now closed) were all named after him. Hester School was built on land bought for $800 from Charles B. Polhemus in 1861.[21] Due to earthquake safety concerns it was rebuilt in 1913, and again in the 1960s.

The Gairaud family's real estate business replaced the Bank of America across the street from Hester School in 1950. Mrs. Irene Gairaud insisted that the new Hester School was not half as strong as the one built in 1913, and despite the fact that Hester School did not meet safety standards, the demolition crew had a hard time tearing down the old school.[22]

The first Hester School in the late 19th century.

The second Hester School, built in 1913.

Tucked away behind these trees is the Moore mansion, which was designed by Theodore Lenzen as a replica of the governor's mansion in Sacramento. This pen and ink drawing is one of the illustrations in the thirty-six-page poem about The Alameda by Mary H. Field, *An Arboreal Song of the Alameda.* It was published in 1878.

California Room

William Squire Clark traveled with the Harlan-Young party from Maryland overland to California. In 1847, he participated in the Battle of Santa Clara. Clark built the first wharf of San Francisco at the Broadway and Battery Street intersection and became a millionaire through San Francisco investments.[23]

4 The Hill/Clark/Leet Property

After 1860, Mrs. Mathilda Hill built one of the largest homes in the city just north of Hester Place, between Schiele Avenue and Pershing Avenue. In 1870, the millionaire William Squire Clark moved to San Jose and built this mansion on the northeast corner of Ninth and Santa Clara Streets. Annoyed by the loud chiming bells of Saint Patrick's Church, Clark felt that he would have a more peaceful existence on The Alameda.[24] Around 1878, Clark purchased the Hill property, dismantled his house, and moved his entire house to The Alameda. Judge John Hendley Moore purchased the existing Hill home on this property and moved it to his property at the corner of Schiele and The Alameda. At the time, the Moore family lived across the street from Mrs. Hill in a square colonial home at the corner of Magnolia Avenue and The Alameda.

In 1921, the Leet family replaced the gorgeous mansion between Schiele and Pershing with another. In November of 1965, the Leet mansion was destroyed by vandals and a fire. The Hill-Clark-Leet property is now occupied by the Bank of America building.

5 The Hill/Moore Mansion

By 1876, there were 14 houses on The Alameda.[25] Judge John Hendley Moore was treasurer of Bishop's San Jose and Santa Clara Railroad in 1868 when they built the horseline along The Alameda.[26] The judge was a proud pioneer and collected western art. Moore owned 14 acres at the corner of Magnolia Avenue and The Alameda. He later moved into a three story Victorian that stood on the corner of Schiele and The Alameda (1600 The Alameda), originally built for Mrs. Mathilda Hill. This home was designed by Theodore Lenzen as an identical copy of the Governer's Mansion in Sacramento. There were several other replicas built, but the Moore residence was the only replica that survived the 1906 earthquake. The mansion had 19 rooms and a ballroom on the third floor. The Moores were known for their elaborate parties, with an infamous punch bowl in the tower room.[27] The mansion stood for almost a century, and even served as a fraternity house for three years before its demolition in 1955.[28]

⑥ The Woodson Property

The Woodson mansion stood at 1061 The Alameda. This home had 15 rooms and two magnolia trees at the entrance that became the two largest magnolia trees in the state of California by 1946.[29]

⑦ The Properties Near W. Julian Street

The Delmas/Morrison House was one of Commodore Stockton's pre-fabricated homes from the East Coast. Sarah and Andrew L. Morrison first lived there in 1866.[30] *The San Jose Mercury* identified Morrison as one of the highest taxpayers in Santa Clara County in 1867. Legend has it that Morrison was deaf, but this did not stop him from collecting tolls at Shartzer's tollgate near Julian Street.[31] Andrew Morrison passed away in 1869, and Sarah Morrison passed away in 1873.[32] James H. Pierce, the owner of the Pacific Manufacturing Company, executed the property and established the Morrison Subdivision around what is now Morrison Avenue. Pierce sold the house to Delphin M. Delmas, who was famous for defending Harry Thaw for the murder of Stanford White in New York.[33]

Samuel Addison Bishop, the father of the San Jose local transit system, moved to The Alameda in 1867. His property was next to Delmas', right before The Alameda curves at Race Street (heading towards Santa Clara). This estate encompassed what used to be the Polhemus' "Maple Hut."

Like the Woodson property, a tree

D. M. Delmas

"Speeches and Addresses" by D. M. Delmas

In a letter to his mother in 1877, student Charles R. Barry noted, "I have been to San Jose today, and had a very pleasant time in the Court House, listening to one of San Jose's best lawyers, Mr. Delmas, a graduate of Santa Clara College…I was completely entranced and came near missing the car for college, for we all must be in before dark."

set a state record for height on this property, too. The eucalyptus tree was planted in 1868, and grew to 148 feet, with a diameter of 86 inches by the time Samuel F. Leib owned the property. Upon his arrival in California, Leib bought a narrow strip of Bishop's land next to his partner at law, Delphin M. Delmas. Leib recalls its planting in a 1939 San Jose Mercury News article, "I was able to establish that date many years after when I ran across the man who helped to plant it. The man told me while he was digging post holes the great earthquake of 1868 occurred and threw him into one of the holes."

Delmas and Bishop, one a famed attorney and the other an innovative entrepreneur, engaged in neighborly competition. When Bishop arrived after the Civil War, Delmas had

Sourisseau Academy

Bishop's marble statue in front of the Bishop home on The Alameda.

RES. OF **THEODORE LENZEN**, ARCHITECT, SAN JOSE, CALIFORNIA.

Thompson & West Historical Atlas

a fountain in his front garden. Bishop out-decorated Delmas by building numerous fountains and even a custom-made statue of himself.[34]

D. M. Delmas' pre-fabricated house burned down in 1879 and the Delmas family moved to San Francisco.[35] The Bishop house burned down in about 1880, but his statue survived and accented his next residence down the street. Leib built a brick mansion on the two properties. He owned the law firm, "Leib & Leib" and was also the vice president of the First National Bank. As a close friend of the Stanfords, Leib protected the University's property from "a multitude of besetting dangers."[36] Eventually, the Leib mansion was destroyed to make way for a 1940s Safeway Store.

(8) Theodore Lenzen

Theodore Lenzen was born in Prussia in 1833 and began the study of architecture at the age of 15. He emigrated to Chicago at the age of 21 to perfect his architectural skills, and arrived in San Francisco in 1861. There, he drew the plans for St. Ignatius College. The next year he came to Santa Clara to design the Santa Clara College. Throughout his career, he designed almost 600 buildings, including the brick St. Joseph's Church (1869), O'Connor Sanitarium at Race and San Carlos, the first Normal School of San Jose (1869), the City Hall (1889), the Fredericksburg Brewery (1883-1891), and the remodel of the Auzerais House (1901), none of which remain standing. Although few of Lenzen's large commercial and public structures still exist, many of the houses he designed are still around to enjoy, including the Kirk Farrington House (1878) on Dry Creek Road and the Scheller-Martin House at San Jose State University (1904). By 1868, Lenzen had purchased a twenty-three acre parcel now bisected by Lenzen Avenue, which he subdivided in the 1870s. He designed and built his own home on the north side of Lenzen Avenue across from Fredericksburg Brewery.[37]

9 Charles M. Schiele

During his lifetime, Charles M. Schiele, was a grocer, waiter, hotel proprietor, miner, as well as a real estate speculator and developer. Born in Germany in 1850, he nearly died of wounds in the Franco-Prussian war. In 1872, he arrived in New York with 35 cents in his pocket. Schiele had another brush with death when he contracted typhoid and brain fever working in the Virginia City silver mines. Upon arriving in San Jose in 1878, he began investing in land. He bought a couple of San Jose hotels, including the Pacific Hotel. He also bought 200 acres of land in Willow Glen. He paid $75,000 for a 15-acre parcel on The Alameda. Schiele had two subdivisions by 1892--one surrounding Schiele Avenue and another surrounding Magnolia Avenue.

10 The Singletary Mansion

Singletary Avenue is named for the Singletary family, who owned the land between Fremont Avenue and Singletary Avenue. Emory C. Singletary, an early pioneer of San Jose, was one of the well-to-do agriculturists of Santa Clara County. This Massachusetts native pursued farming and cattle-raising in Walworth County, Wisconsin. Later, he worked as a cattle dealer in Illinois and Missouri. In 1846, he went to St. Louis to join General Fremont on his western expedition, but promptly returned to Wisconsin after "taking a great dislike to the general." In 1853, he finally traveled to California, accompanied by a party of 19 men. He continued farming and cattle-raising in Colusa and for several years was the largest and best-known cattle dealer in the state. He became one of the largest landholders in the state, at one time holding title to over 35 thousand acres. Five years later he returned to the East Coast and became a horse breeder. In 1873, having sold 9,700 acres of land, Singletary came to the temperate Santa Clara valley to recuperate and regain his health. In 1884 he built a fine residence on Stockton Avenue. He was the first vice president of the First National Bank of San Jose and was one of the directors of the State Agricultural Society for a number of years. He is also noted for being acquainted with Abraham Lincoln. Emory C. Singletary married Florence Grigsby in San Jose and had twins, Emory Grigsby Singletary and George Curtis Singletary.[38] The 1932 city directories list his widow, Florence G. Singletary as living at 1565 the Alameda, George C Singletary at 1585 The Alameda, and Margaret E. Singletary, the widow of Emory G. Singletary, at 1192 Fremont Avenue.

Currently, there are twenty-seven mansions along The Alameda. Most have been turned into businesses. Many mansions were built in the 1920s, and 67 remained in the 1950s.[39] The land values on The Alameda were high in the 1960s, and remodeling the houses into apartments proved difficult. Victorian homes are easier to divide into units because they usually have rooms opening into a common corridor and tend to be based on pattern books. The mansions on The Alameda were customized, with common areas and large entranceways.[40]

Julia Morgan House

⑪ The Julia Morgan House

In 1907, the renowned architect Julia Morgan designed the house at the corner of Villa and The Alameda. J. H. Pierce and his wife, Marian, imported exotic woods from all over the world to build their home, since Pierce's father founded a wood mill—the Pacific Manufacturing Company. Twelve years later, Julia Morgan was hired to design Hearst Castle. When Julia Morgan closed her office in 1951, she ordered the building superintendent to destroy all of her remaining files, records, and drawings. She insisted that "architecture is a visual, not a verbal art."[41] This Julia Morgan house is one of the few that retains its original plans.

⑫ The Dunne Mansion

Possibly the oldest structure on The Alameda, the Victorian mansion on the corner of Emory and The Alameda, has survived since the 1890s. The design of this mansion is attributed to Frank D. Wolfe, a locally acclaimed architect. According to an expert on Wolfe, the architectural details in the house are consistent with those typically found in Wolfe's work. Peter J. Dunne, who inherited great wealth, purchased this mansion in 1901 from James V. Kelly. Peter's parents, James and Catherine Dunne, owned four ranchos and as much as 18,000 acres in Santa Clara Valley and the greater Bay Area.[42]

The Dunne Mansion

13 The Hart Mansion

The Hart mansion is an example of the demolition of a gorgeous 1920s mansion, like many others on The Alameda. Alexander J. Hart, president of L. Hart & Son department store, built the home for $125,000 in 1920. As a gift to his wife Nettie, it was patterned after the Petit Trianon of Versailles. In this house, the Harts received an ominous phone call in 1933 (See box below).

In 1945, an auto dealer purchased the Hart mansion. The mansion housed a chiropractor's office until the city purchased it in 1952 with an ambitious plan to turn it into the "Alexander J. Hart Memorial Center" complete with a museum, art gallery, and library. The city was unable to appropriate the $76,000 needed for the project and therefore sold the property at auction three years later.[47] The YMCA purchased the home and demolished it to make way for the current YMCA building.

14 The James H. Henry Mansion

A historically significant mansion used to stand at the northwest corner of University Avenue and The Alameda. James H. Henry,

This sign can still be seen from Highway 87. The Hart family was one of the wealthiest families in San Jose in the first half of the 20th century.

Brooke Hart, Alexander's son, was the new vice president of L. Hart & Son department store in 1933. Brooke was 22 and had recently graduated from the University of Santa Clara. He was supposed to meet his father in the parking lot of the Hart store to drive him to a Chamber of Commerce dinner, but he failed to arrive.[43] Alexander Hart reported Brooke's disappearance to the police, who in turn broadcasted news of Hart's disappearance on the radio at 9:00 p.m. The kidnappers called the Hart home demanding $40,000 later that night. It was about 9:45 p.m. Brooke's little sister, Eleese, answered the phone, and the kidnappers threatened to kill Brooke if the Harts informed the police. Despite this threat, Alex Hart called the San Jose police chief and phone recording devices were installed in the Hart home. A little after midnight, a Milpitas farmer reported that an automobile resembling Hart's had been standing with its lights on since 6:30 p.m. The next sign of Brooke came two days later, when his wallet was found on the ocean liner, the *Lurline*.[44] A week after Brooke's disappearance, one of the kidnappers called the Hart home with an ultimatum. Alex was to drive towards Los Angeles with the money and exchange it for Brooke. Alex stalled the caller as police traced it and arrived at the phone booth that the kidnapper was using. Thomas H. Thurmond was promptly handcuffed and interrogated. He confessed that he had an accomplice, Jack Holmes. They already had thrown Brooke Hart into San Francisco Bay's mudflats near the San Mateo Bridge. Duck hunters found the body two weeks after the ordeal began.[45] After the body was discovered, a controversial and mysterious San Jose mob formed. The mob broke into the jail where the two kidnappers were detained and lynched them both in St. James Park. The Governor of California stated that he would pardon any convicted member of the "patriotic" mob. No one involved with the lynching was ever arrested.[46]

who established the first electric streetcar with overhead power in California along The Alameda, bought a 200 by 250 foot lot at this location in 1888. He built a magnificent mansion there in 1900. As a result of its building date, it became known as "the Century House."[48] Dr. Pace later bought the mansion and demolished it in the 1970s.

Rose Garden

In 1876, Moses Davis and W. S. Chapman subdivided Poplar City, the location of the current Rose Garden district. The subdivision was bordered by The Alameda, Naglee Avenue, and Park Avenue. By 1915, this area was 75% built-out.[49]

One of the most beautiful parks in the "Garden City" is the San Jose Municipal Rose Garden. Originally, the garden was a 25-acre prune orchard owned by John Crummey. The Santa Clara County Rose Society convinced the city to purchase 5 ½ acres to build the Municipal Rose Garden in 1927. The groundbreaking ceremony for the park was on April 7, 1931. John Crummey was a member of the San Jose Rotary Club, which donated the fountain for the Rose Garden to the city. The Rose Society provided all of the roses. The Rose Garden now consists of 3,500 rose bushes and 189 rose varieties.

John Crummey subdivided the rest of the 25-acre prune orchard in 1937.[50] John Crummey was a generous person and had a tennis court at his home on Park Avenue. All children were welcome to use the tennis court, according to long-time resident Jean Morss. John Crummey was also noted for helping establish the Methodist Church. He began volunteering at the YMCA on South First Street when he was 15 years old and was central in bringing the YMCA to The Alameda in 1955. The Crummey family has always been known for their generosity and community activism in the Rose Garden district.

History San José

This postcard was part of a series published by the San Jose Chamber of Commerce. Its caption reads, "San Jose's Municipal Rose Garden of five and one-half acres, devoted exclusively to plants and shrubs of the 'rose family' is one of the very few municipal rose gardens in the world."

MAP
of the SURVEY of the
CHAPMAN AND DAVIS
TRACT

Surveyed January 1875 by
A. W. Harriman

Shasta-Hanchett Park

Lewis E. Hanchett was a San Jose native, born in 1872. His wealth came from his inherited mining interests in Esmerelda County, Nevada. In 1905, he bought James H. Henry's trolley system for $650,000. In 1906, he added a rail to The Alameda narrow gauge track, making it standard gauge. In the next year, he bought the Agricultural Park and developed the Shasta-Hanchett Park neighborhood, one of San Jose's first "streetcar suburbs." According to its developer at the time, Hanchett Park was "the only subdivision ever placed on the market in California with a modern septic tank sewerage system and flush tanks." Hanchett built a car line from The Alameda to Park Avenue and Race Street via Martin and Tillman Avenues. By 1907, Hanchett had joined Bishop as a "giant of San Jose transit," according to historian Clyde Arbuckle.

The neighborhood was brimming with Craftsman bungalows, Mission style, and Spanish Eclectic style architecture by the 1930s. Currently, Shasta-Hanchett Park has the area's largest collection of craftsman houses built between 1900 and 1920. (See page 100 for more information about Shasta-Hanchett Park in the Hanchett Residence Park Walking History Tour)

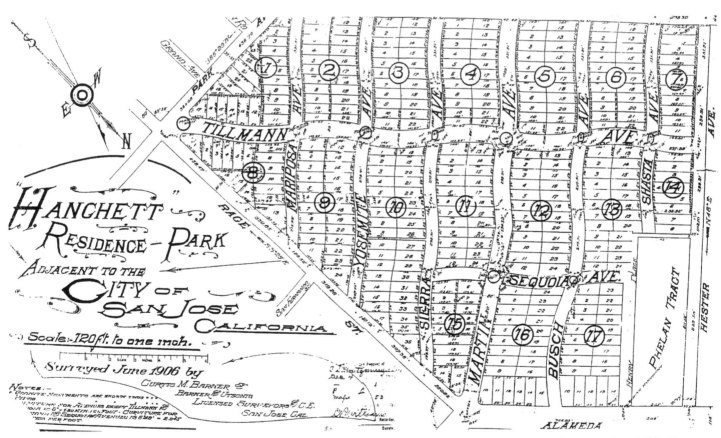

First American Title Company

College Park was annexed by San Jose on November 24, 1925. At that time, the College Park district encompassed the Rose Garden and Hanchett Park.[51] Elections were held to annex College Park four times, and not until the fourth try did the City have success. The 1925 annexation added 15,000 people to San Jose's population, and increased San Jose's area by one-third. Proponents of the annexation celebrated with a huge bonfire on The Alameda, on a lot owned by an opponent to the annexation named Hiram Blanchard. The celebration also included a band that played, "Hail, Hail, the Gang's All Here!"[52]

This map is dated August 25, 1866, and the land was surveyed by the J. J. Bowden Company. The streets Asbury, Emory, Hedding, "McKendre" (now McKendrie), and Hamline were named for Methodist bishops.

Education

University of the Pacific—College Park

The Methodist Church conferred on Reverend Edward Bannister the task of establishing the first chartered college in California. At the time, Bannister served as a professor at the Cazinovia Seminary in New York. Almost immediately after arriving in California, Bannister became principal of the San Jose Academy on the southeast corner of Second and San Fernando Streets.[1] Quarterly tuition began at $10. Weekly board was $7.[2] On July 10, 1851, the California Supreme Court chartered the California Wesleyan College. This name was common among Methodist colleges all over the country, and proved unpopular. At its first meeting, the Board of Trustees decided to change the name to "The University of the Pacific." Years later, one of the founders reflected, "Why not plant the germ of a University and give it a big name to grow up to and into? Sure enough, why not? And give the name we did, half-laughing and half prophesying as we did it."[3]

Isaac Owen is credited as founder of The University of the Pacific, though he was never its president. He arrived in California in 1849 with similar aspirations as Bannister, and was responsible for raising funds when the college was first chartered. His tenacity and passion for education led some to believe that if he had it his way, there would be a "high school at every crossroad and a college in every county."[4]

The University of the Pacific campus was relocated to Santa Clara on what is now called Main Street.[5] Classes commenced in a small two-story building on May 3, 1852. The charter for University of the Pacific preceded that of Mission School (Santa Clara University) and the College of Notre Dame by a few months.

In 1858, the University of the Pacific founded the first medical school in the state. Located in San Francisco, the school had shaky beginnings due to the Civil War, and was

Reverend Edward Bannister

Sourisseau Academy

First College in California?

The charter for the "California Wesleyan College" was granted on July 10, 1851, making it the first college to receive a charter in the state of California. However, the foundation of "Mission School" (Santa Clara University) was laid in March of 1851, before the Methodists chose their square mile of land on which they would build The University of the Pacific.[6]

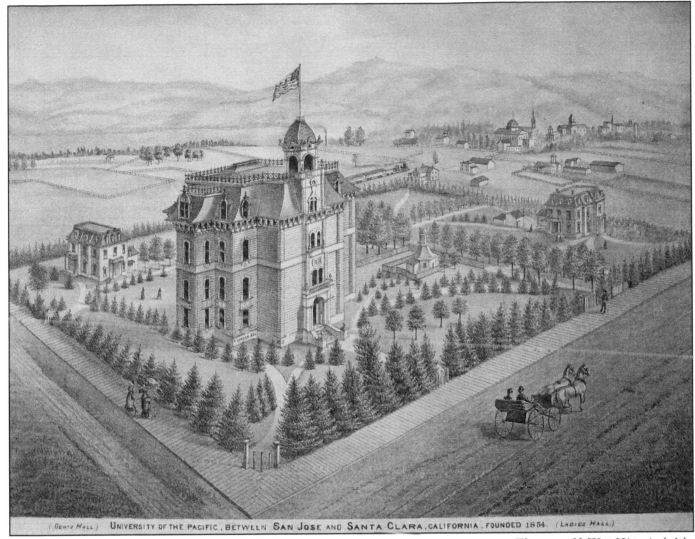

Thompson & West Historical Atlas

This pen and ink sketch depicts West Hall, which was the first of the University of the Pacific's seven buildings.

closed between 1864 and 1870. Meanwhile, the University of California organized its School of Medicine--the Toland Medical College.[7] Due to intense competition, the Medical College at the University of the Pacific was dissolved and incorporated as the Cooper Medical School of San Francisco, which later became the Medical Department of Stanford University.

When the University of the Pacific was first organized, it was resolved that admission be open to women. The "Female Collegiate Institute" was officially organized in 1853, with Mrs. Bannister as Preceptress. At the Female Institute, the curriculum included embroidery, painting, and "hair work," which included "weaving into intricate floral patterns locks of the hair of one's relatives and friends."[8]

In the spring of 1858, the first class to graduate "in a classical course in California" included Thomas Laine, Joseph C. Hamer, John W. Owen, DeWitt Vestal, Elijah Hook, Martha J. Hughes, Mary A. Miller, Mary B. McDonald, Emeline Brickett and Mary Smith.[9] The male and female departments received their diplomas separately. The female graduation took place at the old adobe church, and the male graduation took place at Cook's Pond.[10]

The male and female departments remained separate and the issue of whether to unite the male and female departments was a topic of hot debate. In 1854, the trustees ordered that the departments be united, but in 1856 they were separated again. The Female

To the far left is the Jackson-Goodstall Astronomical Observatory. In the middle-left stands West Hall, which was built in 1871 as a ladies dormitory. To the right, East Hall served as the men's dormitory and was designed by Levi Goodrich. Classes began in College Park in 1872.[11]

Department was finally incorporated into the main University in 1869.[12]

In 1866, in an effort to secure the financial future of the college, the trustees of the University of the Pacific purchased 432 acres on the northeast side of The Alameda to subdivide the University Tract around a new campus. Construction of the homes did not pick up pace until the college campus and electric streetcar were well established. By 1915, craftsman-style houses were well represented in College Park, many of which still remain today.[13]

University officials attempted to name the College Park district, "University Park." Unfortunately, this title was already taken by University of Southern California. University of the Pacific had to settle for the name "College Park." Decades later, William Guth convinced trustees that "University" was a presumptuous title, and the University of the Pacific became College of the Pacific. The name did not did not revert to "University" again until 1961.[14]

In 1910, the trustees purchased seven acres of land on The Alameda and the president of the University, Dr. William Wesley Guth, moved into a mansion on the northwest corner of Emory and The Alameda. Presidents Dr. John L. Seaton and Dr. Tully C. Knoles later occupied the 14-room mansion. It was eventually razed.[15]

In 1921, the University of Pacific ran into financial trouble. Both Central Hall and West Hall burned down in 1914 and trustees disliked the noisy railroad. Also, competition for students was intense, with Santa Clara

History San José

East Hall had four floors before the earthquake of 1906, but after extensive earthquake damage the University of The Pacific had to remove the top floor and strengthen the rest.

William A. Wulf

CONSERVATORY OF MUSIC

Organized in 1878, the University of the Pacific Conservatory of Music was the first of its kind west of the Mississippi River. The Conservatory Building was built on the College Park Campus in 1890.

DORMITORY BUILDING
UNIVERSITY OF THE PACIFIC
SAN JOSE, CAL.

William A. Wulf

This two-story stucco building was built in 1911 during the time when William Guth was president of the College of the Pacific. It was named Helen Guth Hall, after Guth's wife, and was used as a women's dormitory. It later became part of Bellarmine's campus.

University, Stanford University, and University of California, Berkeley, all in close proximity. The offer to move the campus to the City of Stockton was irresistible.[16] The new Stockton campus was dedicated in 1925. That year, the Santa Clara "Prep" School moved to the College Park Campus. In 1926, this school was renamed the Bellarmine College Preparatory. The University of Pacific officially sold the four remaining blocks of the University Tract to Bellarmine in 1928.[17]

Bellarmine College Preparatory

Bellarmine College Preparatory is arguably the oldest private high school in the State of California. Bellarmine was an offshoot of the Jesuit Santa Clara College, founded by Father John Nobili in 1851. What came to be known as the Santa Clara University originally catered to elementary, secondary, and college-age students. The elementary grades were discontinued in 1903. In 1912, Santa Clara College was renamed as two separate schools—Santa Clara University and Santa Clara Preparatory. This secondary school opened doors to its first 200 students in 1926. The Archbishop of San Francisco, Edward Joseph Hanna, suggested that the school honor Robert Cardinal Bellarmine, a Jesuit of the sixteenth century. Robert Cardinal Bellarmine had recently been canonized a saint and recognized as a Doctor of the Church. Thus, the Santa Clara Preparatory was renamed the Bellarmine College Preparatory in 1926. The name change was accompanied by a change in school colors, from red and white to blue and white, to honor the Virgin Mary.[18] Now, Bellarmine has an enrollment of over 1,500 students.

Jack Kerouac passed Bellarmine every day when he worked in the trainyards. He referenced the school in his book, *Lonesome Traveler*, in a piece titled, "October in the Railroad Earth."

Lincoln High School, located on Dana Avenue, is known for having the oldest high school rivalry in the State of California. In 1945, Lincoln High School played San Jose High in the first annual football game known as the Big Bone Game. This game acquired its name when a San Jose High student found a large steer leg in his father's butcher shop and declared it the trophy for the winning school. Rex Kuehner remembers when his sister, Jo Ellen Kuehner, won the title as the Big Bone Queen in 1961. She was the number one cheerleader at the time. Lincoln lost that year, but in 1962, Lincoln began its longest winning streak in Big Bone history, which lasted until 1969. Lincoln and San Jose High Academy continue to compete for the Big Bone at San Jose City College every Thanksgiving Day.

First English School

The first English school in California opened at Mission Santa Clara in 1847. Mrs. Olive Mann Isbell served as the school's only teacher. She was the niece of Horace Mann, "the father of the American common school," who founded the first public school system in Massachusetts in 1837.

Olive and her husband, Isaac Chauncey Isbell, left Greenbush, Illinois on April 17, 1846 and began their journey over the great American plains. When they reached Fort Hall in present-day Idaho, they heard that the Californios were threatening to kill all American immigrants. Her husband, Isaac Chauncey Isbell, asked her, "What shall we do, Olive dearest?" Olive's fearless response was, "I started for California, and I want to go on. Can't we, James?"[19]

Joseph Aram, the soon-to-be captain of Northern California, accompanied them to Sacramento Valley. There, they agreed to continue to Sutter's Fort on October 1, 1846, led by Colonel Fremont. As a surgeon and a nurse, the couple was needed at Mission Santa Clara. Mexican General Sanchez and his army were threatening to seize the mission. They heroically proceeded to Mission Santa Clara as reinforcements. They arrived just before the Battle of Santa Clara and found the Mission in great confusion. The men who joined Fremont's division left their families to be cared for at the mission. A total of 175 resided at the mission, and many were ill from typhoid. Olive cared for the sick, dressed wounds, and prepared meals for soldiers.[20] In December, 1846, Olive described the situation at the mission, "… almost every one sick, without care; most of the men in the lower country with Fremont; surrounded by Californians, expecting every day to be attacked by them…"[21]

At the Battle of Santa Clara, Captain Marsten borrowed Olive Mann's wedding handkerchief for a peace flag to call a truce.[22] During the uprising at the mission, 14 people

The Battle of Santa Clara

The Battle of Santa Clara was the only American skirmish in northern California during the Mexican-American war. The actual battle was two hours long, but 5 days of negotiations ensued before the official treaty ceremony. Carlos María Weber, a Prussian-Mexican citizen, was appointed by Commodore Stockton as sergeant of the San Jose Militia. In 1846, Weber and his men began raiding the horse and cattle corrals of rancheros in the Valley, including those at the Sanchez Rancho. Consequently, Francisco Sanchez became the head of a band of up to over 100 angry Californios, who blamed the Americans for the raids. Captain Joseph Aram, given charge in the north by Colonel Fremont, organized a company of 36 men to come to San Jose. Aram didn't help matters when Aram chopped down several sacred willow trees from The Alameda to barricade the mission, despite the pleas of the Californios.[23]

The "battle" commenced on the second of January 1847, and ended on the seventh. The United States forces, led by Captain Carlos María Weber and Captain Ward Marston, caught word of the Californio insurgents on their way to Mission Santa Clara. As they approached the Mexican forces, they could see Mission Santa Clara three miles ahead over a low oak forest. The Americans' advance was delayed when their cannon got stuck in mud, but they continued on to the mission after extracting the cannon. They fought in an open plain near what is now Lawrence Expressway. Grove Cook, a so-called "Indian fighter and trapper," recalled, "Yep, the Battle of Santa Clara, both sides fit like hell all day to keep from getting within two miles of each other."[24] According to another witness, the soldiers were "more interested in making noise than hitting anyone."[25] As people watched from mission rooftops, there was gunfire, and the rancheros retreated to the mountains. Both newspapers reported that no one was killed or wounded on either side. It is said that Francisco Sanchez sent James Alexander Forbes, a Scot by birth, to call a truce and end the battle.

died, mostly of typhoid.

To keep the children occupied during this hard time, Olive Mann Isbell opened the first English school. Thomas O. Larkin, Milton Little, and H.T. Green sponsored the enterprise, and each scholar was charged $2 per month. Isbell taught in a small adobe at Mission Santa Clara. This adobe was originally a home for Mission personnel, then a stable. After 1836, the comisionado probably kept his personal horses there.

Light and ventilation in the 11 x 18 foot classroom was limited to a hole in the roof. Olive Mann Isbell had limited teaching resources. With no paper or ink, she used a long pointed stick to teach the three Rs on the dirt floor, and students used charcoal to write the ABCs on the palms of their hands.

Mrs. Isbell became affectionately known as "Aunt Olive," despite the rudimentary conditions.[26] The school opened at the beginning of 1847 with 25 pupils, and housed 56 at the end of three months. In the spring, Isbell moved to Monterey and opened a school there. The historical adobe became a stable again after her departure, as noted in an 1854 survey map, but in 1850 a permanent school opened on Lexington street.

The Alameda Attractions

Rose Carnival

Six years after the first flower-bedecked horses and carriages paraded down the streets of Pasadena, San Jose held its first Carnival of Roses in 1896. It lasted four days and probably included a parade. On the fourth day the Garden City Cyclers held a competition for which they advertised, "All the Coast Crackajacks will Ride." What first transpired on the 6th of May, 1896 quickly became a San Jose tradition.

This was the medallion designed in honor of the first Rose Parade Queen in 1896, Lillian Rea.

In honor of President McKinley's 1901 visit, the City of San Jose planned a parade along The Alameda. Every float in the parade was covered with roses. Float sponsors included clubs, schools, ranches, religious institutions, and parks. President McKinley gave a speech on May 13th and reviewed the floats.[1] Unfortunately, Mrs. McKinley fell ill and McKinley and his party left before the parade.[2] Nonetheless, the carnival was a jubilant event.

A third Rose Carnival took place in 1910. This one consisted of a "Santa Clara College Day," a "Santa Clara County Day" and an "Aviation Day." A "Grand Spectacular Evening Parade" was held at 8:00 P.M. on the second night, with a Mardi-Gras theme and illuminated floats. The brochure advertised a grand masked ball, confetti, and fire works. During this particular festival, the parade did not travel down The Alameda.

As she encouraged the city to hold a fourth Rose Carnival, Mrs. Fremont Older pointed out, "The Spanish government established San Jose in 1777 for a vegetable garden. It is the Garden city. Let us prove it."

From the Bouquet to the Reviewing Stand.

California Room

Two thousand women of Santa Clara County contributed to a single, massive bouquet of flowers for President McKinley. Mrs. E. O. Smith (to the right of McKinley) presented the flowers to him. President McKinley received his bouquet of roses exactly four months before he was assassinated.

Float "Temple of Vesta," University of the Pacific.

Rose Carnival, 1901.

California Room

Float "Copa de Oro," Hester School.

Rose Carnival, 1901.   *California Room*

MAY
11-12-13-14
19 10
SANTA CLARA CO. ROSE CARNIVAL,
SAN JOSE CAL

COPYRIGHT 1910. WEBB DRUG CO.

History San José

The Rose Carnival became Fiesta de Las Rosas in 1926. Older directed a committee charged with planting thousands of rose bushes donated by nurseries and individuals. During the years of the Fiesta de Las Rosas, schoolyards, service stations, gardens, empty lots, and street corners were bedecked with roses. From the 2,000 slogan ideas submitted, the committee chose "Santa Clara Valley, the Rose Garden of the World."

The streets in downtown San Jose were decorated with flags and banners, and the clerks in the stores wore Spanish costumes. In the "Grand Floral Parade," 87 floats, 14 decorated cars, 10 bands and more than 200 mounted riders marched down The Alameda, starting at the Mission Santa Clara and ending in the Pueblo de San Jose de Guadalupe.

All of the carnivals lasted a couple of days and attracted a quarter of a million spectators. Each festival featured an original play based on early California produced by the students, faculty, staff, and families of San Jose State University. One festival included a Shakespeare garden exhibit with all of the flowers mentioned in Shakespeare's works.

The seventh carnival took place in 1932. The Fiestas were discontinued due to the Depression until the city revived the Fiesta in 1969. This final Rose Carnival included a parade, a pageant, fandangos, sports events, a great west rodeo, a rose show, and a horse show.[3]

The Agricultural Park

The Santa Clara Valley Agricultural Society began having state fairs in 1856, but lacked a permanent, designated land parcel. Hiram Shartzer, who set up the toll road on The Alameda in 1862, was on the committee to purchase permanent land for the fair in 1859. The committee sold subscriptions and raised $14,464.55 in two weeks. Having paid General Naglee

History San José

Pioneers, Agricultural Park June 23ᵈ 1900. Tucker

History San José

This is a plaque depicting one of Stanford's racehorse, "Occident." The plaque says,

" The California Wonder OCCIDENT
owned by Gov L. Stanford
Time in harness a private trial of
speed
2:19 2:19 2:19 "

$6,000 for the 76-acre parcel, plenty of extra funding remained to improve the park. This land at the bend of The Alameda between Race Street and Hester Street served as a recreational spot for over 40 years. Livestock fairs, circuses, and fancy-dress balls in the Pink Pavilion (also known as the Rose Carnival Pavilion) made this one of the most popular San Jose parks.[4] Exhibitions ranged from fruit and livestock to pianos and quilts.[5]

Leland Stanford raced his prize horses, Palo Alto and Occident, at the racetrack in the Agricultural Park. After returning from his trip around the world in 1879, President Grant visited The Agricultural Park to watch Occident race against the clock.[6]

The Agricultural Park had two racing venues—a racetrack and a bicycle velodrome. Many famous cyclists competed in the Agricultural Park's quarter-mile concrete velodrome. In 1890, bicycling became one of the most competitive sports in San Jose. Clubs included the Garden City Wheelmen, the San Jose Road Club, and the Elite Cyclers. (For more information about velodromes, see page 120)

"Safety" bicycles began to replace the high-wheelers in the 1890s. In 1896, there was a bicycle boom in America, especially evident in San Jose. Terence Shaw of The Garden City Cyclists (formerly "Wheelmen") explains, "Bicycling used to be a bigger sport in America than baseball and San Jose was one of the hotbeds, major league cities. The whole town was involved in racing."[7]

On the 20th of November 1894, the following petition was signed by over 20 residents on The Alameda, including A. L. Rhodes, E. L. Dawson (son of J. M. Dawson and co-founder of the J. M. Dawson Packing Co.), and Mrs. Bishop:

To the Honorable Board of Supervisors of Santa Clara County

Gentlemen,
We the undersigned residents on and near the Alameda Avenue would say; the side walks of said Alameda Avenue are to a great extent monopolized by bicycle riders, and in view of the fact, that a new bicycle track will shortly be completed at the Race Track, which will greatly increase the number of bicycle riders riding on the side walks of said Alameda Avenue, and that as the riding on said side walks is a constant source of danger to life and comfort of pedestrians. We would therefore respectfully request, that some action be taken by your Honorable Body, to prevent bycicle [sic] riding on side walks of said Alameda Avenue.[8]

Gentlemen:

We the undersigned residents on and near the Alameda Avenue would say; the side walks of said Alameda Avenue are to a great extent monopolized by bicycle riders, and in view of the fact, that a new bicycle track will shortly be completed at the Race Track, which will greatly increase the number of bicycle riders riding on the side walks of said Alameda Avenue, and that as the riding on said side walks is a constant source of danger to life and comfort of pedestrians. We would therefore respectfully request, that some action be taken by your Honorable Body, to prevent bycicle riding on side walks of said Alameda Avenue. And will ever pray that our request be granted.

This is the only known picture of the cement velodrome at the Agricultural Park. Note the castle-like Fredericksburg Brewery in the background.

Leonard McKay

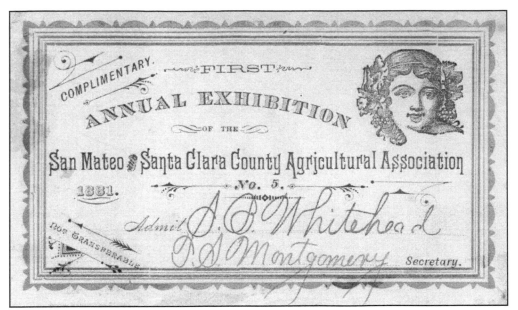

This is a ticket of admission to the first annual exhibition at the Agricultural Park under the direction of the San Mateo & Santa Clara Agricultural Association.

In 1880, the legislature passed an act dividing California into agricultural districts. The San Mateo and Santa Clara Agricultural Association replaced the Agricultural Society in operating The Agricultural Park. For decades, the state had provided a yearly subsidy of $2,000 to maintain the park, but after the reorganization, the state stopped providing subsidies.[9]

Due to a lack of funding and the accumulation of debts, the last state fair was held around 1900. The land was sold to the Peninsula Land and Development Company, headed by Louis E. Hanchett, in 1901. Racing continued in the park before Hanchett began developments there. In 1903, Barney Oldfield broke the world's auto speed record in the racetrack, reaching 60 miles per hour.

Rosicrucian Park

The Rosicrucian Order dates back to the 15th century. The Ancient Mystical Order Rosae Crucis (AMORC) was incorporated as an American institution in 1915 as the modern incarnation of a millennias-old tradition. From 1915 to 1927 the administrative center was in New York City, then in San Francisco, and then in Tampa. The Order found its permanent home in San Jose in 1927. Since then, Rosicrucian Park has been a San Jose landmark and the focus of Rosicrucian activity in North America.

Dr. H. Spencer Lewis was the first world leader of AMORC (Ancient Mystical Order Rosae Crucis) and a figure central to the development of the Rosicrucian Museum. In 1921, he encouraged order members to support the Egypt Explorations Society in Tel el Amarna, the sacred city of Pharaoh Akhenaten. As a result, the Society donated several artifacts from their finds. These artifacts contributed to the original "Rosicrucian Egyptian Oriental Museum," dedicated in 1932.

Dr. Lewis owned a single lot at the corner of Naglee and The Alameda. Even when there was only a mansion on the lot he termed it "Rosicrucian Park." According to Grand Secretary Frater Harvey Miles, when Dr. Lewis was asked how he could call a single lot a "Park," he would reply, "Because that is the way I see it will be in the future."

Lewis' vision of the future was soon realized. As Rosicrucian Park spread further over the city block, the Order's cultural and educational facilities expanded. The Francis Bacon Auditorium, largest in San Jose for many years, was dedicated in 1931, followed by the Rose-Croix University in 1934, the Planetarium in 1936, the Rose-Croix Research Institute and Clinic in 1938, and the research Library in 1939. Dr. Lewis also dreamed of erecting a temple that would honor all aspects of Rosicrucian spiritual life. This dream became a reality when the Supreme Temple was built in 1949.

Ralph M. Lewis, AMORC's second Imperator, opened a new museum building in 1966. This museum houses the largest display of Egyptian artifacts in the Western United States. It is said that this is the only such museum in existence designed in the Egyptian style and situated in an Egyptian Revival park.[10]

Today, Rosicrucian Park continues to serve as the headquarters of the English Grand Lodge for the Americas for AMORC.

History San José

This postcard reads: "This is a replica of the original shrine built in early history in the Temple of Karnak in Egypt. The shrine shown is located in Rosicrucian (Amorc) Park, San Jose."

History San José

This postcard reads: "Headquarters of the North and South America jurisdiction of the Rosicrucian order. In the Park there is maintained for research and for the public a planetarium and museum. The Rosicrucian Egyptian and Oriental Museum contains one of the largest collections west of the Mississippi and one of the outstanding Egyptian collections in the United States." (For more information about AMORC, see page 127)

Innovation and Industries

John J. Montgomery

John Joseph Montgomery (1858-1911) was one of the greatest aeronautic scientists at the turn of the century. His discoveries in airplane technology include cambered wings and the "Montgomery gyroscope."

Montgomery attended Santa Clara University in 1874 and graduated from St. Ignatius College in 1880. For some, Montgomery's flight attempt of 1883 earned him the title, "father of basic flying." At Otay Mesa, San Diego County, Montgomery flew 600 feet in a glider that he designed. This was a decade before the Wright brothers' historic flight. It was the first successful controlled flight in a heavier-than-air vessel.

Between 1883 and 1889 Montgomery used water currents to study curved surfaces. He was invited back to Santa Clara University in 1896, where he taught part time and experimented with model planes. From his experiments, Montgomery determined that the best wing structure "is one having a gradually increasing curvature from the rear to the front edge."[1] This theory led to his 1906 patent for cambered wings, a design upon which all modern planes are constructed.

On April 29, 1905, Montgomery demonstrated his first public high air flight in the vineyard of Santa Clara University. A hot air balloon carried Montgomery's glider, *The Santa Clara*, 4,000 feet into the sky, piloted by Dan Maloney. Twenty minutes later, Maloney landed in the wheat field of the Santa Clara Mill and Lumber Company—a company located on The Alameda. No previous flight attempt had exceeded a height 15 feet above the ground.

Montgomery's next public demonstration took place in The Agricultural Park on May 21, 1905. Maloney ascended twice from the racetrack, first in *The Santa Clara* and then in *The California*, carried by Frank Hamilton's hot air balloon. Both flight attempts were technical and financial failures as a result of mass confusion. An unauthorized person opened a rear gate to the park, collecting money illegally from 1,000 spectators. Amidst this confusion, a person pretending to be a mechanic for Montgomery loosened bolts on *The California*. Also, at the last minute, Frank Hamilton became angry when Montgomery

A cloth advertising banner designed by Richard E. Montgomery for his brother's aircraft demonstration at The Agricultural Park.

Plant 51

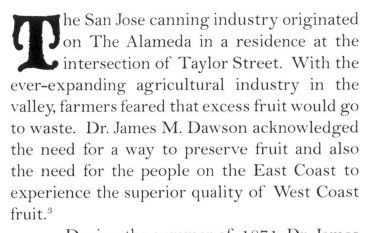

Santa Clara University Archives

In 1905, this hot-air balloon carried Dan Maloney 4,000 feet into the sky, where he was cut loose and glided successfully to a predesignated location near The Alameda.

The San Jose canning industry originated on The Alameda in a residence at the intersection of Taylor Street. With the ever-expanding agricultural industry in the valley, farmers feared that excess fruit would go to waste. Dr. James M. Dawson acknowledged the need for a way to preserve fruit and also the need for the people on the East Coast to experience the superior quality of West Coast fruit.[3]

During the summer of 1871, Dr. James M. Dawson and his family packed 350 cases of canned fruit in a 12x16 woodshed behind their home. They sold the canned peaches, apricots, pears, and plums to the J. K. Armsby Company in San Francisco. The next year they bought their own 50-acre orchard at 16th and Julian Streets. Dawson took his brother-in-law, W. S. Stevens, as partner and they packed 1,000 cases. Dawson's success led to the formation of the San Jose Fruit Packing Company in 1873. As a doctor, J. M Dawson was a pioneer in hygenic canning. Long before Upton Sinclaire's book, *The Jungle*, J. M. Dawson stressed the importance of a clean packing environment. In 1878 J. M. Dawson and his son, Earnest L. Dawson, sold their interests in the San Jose Fruit Packing Company to start another J. M. Dawson Packing Company at their original site on The Alameda.[4] After J. M. Dawson passed away in 1885, his older son, Thomas Benton Dawson became the superintendent of the Cutting Fruit Packing Company in San Francisco. Thomas Dawson rejoined the San Jose Fruit Packing Company when it merged into the Cutting Fruit Packing Company in 1899. Thomas Dawson later became the first general superintendent of the California Packing Corporation, which included the Del Monte Plant 51 packing plant on The Alameda.[5]

would not allow him to pilot *The Santa Clara*. Consequently, Hamilton demanded $500 from Montgomery to use his balloon. Just before Maloney ascended into the sky, Montgomery and Maloney were forced to sacrifice their entire revenue from entrance fees to pay Hamilton the $500 usage fee.[2]

The Santa Clara detached from the balloon too early and Maloney glided down from 150 feet. During the second flight attempt in *The California*, Maloney noticed the loose bolts at the height of 1,000 feet so he did not detach the glider from the balloon. Forty-five minutes later, Maloney landed 30 miles away, near Gilroy, with the balloon still attached.

Dr. J. M. Dawson   *Eugene T. Sawyer*

J M Dawson

Calpak was the first canner to nationally advertise and distribute its products under the single brand name of Del Monte. Calpak introduced the industry's first organized agricultural and scientific programs. As one of seven Calpak plants in San Jose, Plant 51 was an integral element in the local development of the California Packing Corporation. Santa Clara County was producing 90 percent of California's canned food in the 1940s.[6] The Calpak District Manager operated all seven plants from his office building on The Alameda, the small brick building nestled between White and Bush Streets. Plant 51 closed in 1990, and is currently being redeveloped as residential town homes.

Distinguished Women

emale innovators on The Alameda are frequently overlooked. Lucy A. Corning, Dr. Euthanasia A. Meade and Dr. Elizabeth Gallimore all made their mark in history in the neighborhoods surrounding The Alameda. Lucy A. Corning, lived near The Alameda with her husband Thomas Corning (a horse-trainer, probably at the Agricultural Park) when she invented and patented the baling press in 1881.

The first two female physicians in San Jose lived on The Alameda—Euthanasia A. Meade and Elizabeth Gallimore. They set up practice together on The Alameda in 1889 in a Victorian mansion on the northeast corner of the University intersection. Meade lived three blocks away, near Randol Street on The Alameda. These women were the first to prove to San Jose that women could be physicians as well as men. In his book written in 1888, Foote included a biography of Euthanasia Meade among biographies of many prominent men of Santa Clara County.

Sourisseau Academy

The Gallimore residence once stood at 1860 The Alameda.

Foote states,

> Yet what more fitting than that she who best knows how to soothe the moments of anguish and pain should also watch over and destroy the seeds of disease, and check and alleviate the pangs of suffering and distress. Above all things a physician must be wise tender, and sympathetic, and it is in these very provinces that woman is supreme. Hence it is that we hail with joy the enlarging of the mental vision of our days which permits woman to take her proper station by the bedside of illness and disease as a physician.

Dr. Elizabeth Gallimore worked with Euthanasia Meade for three years towards the end of Euthanasia's life. Born in 1863 near what is now Moffet Field, Gallimore is noted as the first female native of Santa Clara Valley to become a physician. She graduated from University of the Pacific and received her medical diploma from Cooper Medical College in San Francisco in 1887.[7]

The Fredericksburg Brewery

One of the most popular attractions on The Alameda at the turn of the century was the Fredericksburg Brewery and Resort. In 1869, Gottfried Frederick Krahenberg, a German tavern keeper, set up a brewery in a small brick shanty on the corner of The Alameda and Cinnabar Street. Theodore Lenzen designed a huge brick brew

FREDERICKSBURG BREWERY.
KRAHENBERG & CO. PROPRIETORS.

Thompson & West Historical Atlas

The Fredricksburg Restaurant and Resort was built around one of the houses that Stockton brought from the East Coast to The Alameda. Note the outline of this house behind the "Fredericksburg Restaurant" sign. Beneath the first-floor overhang, the Fredericksburg Restaurant advertises, "Meals 25 cents, sandwiches, 10 cents." (ca. 1885)

Sourisseau Academy

In 1891, the Fredericksburg Brewery was known for having the largest malt house in the United States.

and malt house to replace the shanty in 1872. The Fredericksburg Brewery became one of the largest breweries in Santa Clara Valley. At first, the brewery produced 4,000 to 5,000 barrels of beer per year, and 53,000 barrels per year by 1888.[8] The Fredericksburg's advertisement was simple: "It is the best."[9]

In 1890, a British syndicate bought The Fredericksburg Brewery. Even after a 1902 fire destroyed the malt house, it continued to be known as "the biggest pile of bricks in town."[10] The castle-like turrets of the Brewery fell during the earthquake of 1906. In 1952, *California Today* noted that the Fredericksburg "withstood the earthquake of 1906 but could not survive Prohibition."[11] After 1918, it was closed. Until the prohibition laws were repealed in 1933, James A Talbot tried to operate the brewery, producing "near beer," only to lose money.[12] The Pacific Brewing and Malting Company purchased the Brewery in 1936. The Fredericksburg label was used until 1939, when it was relabeled Wieland's Beer.

In 1952, the Falstaff Brewing Corporation bought the Pacific Brewing and Malting Company. Falstaff produced six million cases each year on The Alameda, but unfortunately for The Alameda, this was not enough to meet demand. Operations were consolidated in San Francisco, where the company was able to produce twenty million cases a year. The San Jose plant was torn down in 1980.[13]

The Fredericksburg Brewery in 1875.

History San José

William A. Wulf

A mustache comb souvenir from the Fredericksburg Brewery and Resort.

Leonard McKay

The Fredericksburg Brewery on fire in 1902. The photo is titled, "A Critical Moment."

Cheim Lumber Company

San Jose hit a new high in monthly fire loss when the Cheim Lumber Company caught fire in 1951. The Cheim Lumber Company at the corner of Lenzen and The Alameda was adjacent to the streetcar barns and Wieland's Brewery (originally the Fredericksburg Brewery). A janitor discovered the fire among piles of waste paper and scrap wood in the mill, but by the time the fire department arrived the fire had blazed out of control. Sixty firefighters, including 25 off-shift, fought the fire. Six thousand spectators gathered to see the flames, including the patrons of the Towne Theater, whose movie was interrupted when utility crews cut off the power in the area.

On April 14, 1955, another fire plagued this area. The Cheim Lumber Company used a small shed behind the mill to store window glass. A couple of small boys found their way into this shed and were playing with matches that they stole from Franco's Grocery. The shed caught fire, and so did the carbarn. The heat from this fire was so intense that it cracked store windows in the vicinity and melted a streetlight electrolier across the street. Some of the carbarns were then occupied by the Pacific Hardware and Steel Company, which also caught fire. By this time, the firefighters were fighting with a burned hose. Seventy-seven firemen, including 33 off-shift firemen, fought the blaze this time. Noreen Martin recalls her father, an employee of the Falstaff Brewery (formerly Wieland's), fighting the fire from a tower at the brewery, determined to rescue Falstaff from the flames. They managed to save the brewery and Franco's Grocery store across the street, but the fire damaged the Prime Rib restaurant.[14]

Smith & McKay Printing Company

On April 15, 1955, a fire that began in the rear of the Cheim Lumber Company yard, spread to the Pacific Hardware & Steel Company store, and gutted the Prime Rib dining room next door.

William A. Wulf

Lumber

During the gold rush, prices for goods in California soared—especially in the lumber industry. Lumber was crucial to the development of San Jose. Because of the proximity of both Los Gatos Creek and the railroad, The Alameda had a thriving lumber industry. The lumber floated down the Los Gatos Creek from the Santa Cruz Mountains. The Santa Clara Valley Mill and Lumber Company had multiple planing mills and storage yards on The Alameda, where Montgomery's historic glider landing took place. Other lumber companies surrounding The Alameda included Garden City Lumber, the Hubbard and Carmichael Lumber Yard, and the Alameda Lumber Company (also known as the S. H. Chase Lumber Company).

Mills

Around 1854, Santa Clara County had the highest wheat production in California, with 22,745 cultivated acres. The county was the third largest center for milling flour, with San Francisco holding the title of "milling center." Santa Clara County's seven mills could produce five hundred barrels of grain per day, producing almost 30% of California's wheat.[15]

In the early days, The Alameda's *zanjas* provided the City of Santa Clara a waterflow to use for a mill. In her comprehensive review, *Flour Milling in Santa Clara Valley*, Charlene Detlefs [Duval] states,

> The City of Santa Clara may have had an adobe water-powered mill during this period. It was probably located just north of Cook's Pond, near where the Alameda, Bellomy, and Grant Streets converge, and operated on water supplied by Cook's Pond (The Pozo) or the Mission zanja (irrigation ditch) that ran along the Alameda.

Many Alameda residents invested in the Santa Clara milling industry. In the 1830s, George Fergusun built one of the earliest non-commercial mills across the Guadalupe River from The Alameda, near San Fernando Street. Don Antonio Suñol bought this mill in 1841.

Charles Clayton and Samuel J. Johnson opened the Santa Clara Steam Mill in 1852, which drew water from Cook's Pond on the

2863 - ''The Old Stone Mill'' - erected 1850. First Building in Los Gatos. California.

History San José

corner of Bellomy Street and The Alameda. This mill was reputed to be the first steam flour mill in California. After this "Old Adobe" gristmill was destroyed in a fire, it was relocated to Grant Street in 1878. Farmer's Mill replaced the "Old Adobe" Santa Clara Steam Mill on The Alameda.

James Alexander Forbes (see page 26) built one of the first large commercial mills in Santa Clara Valley—Forbes Mill in Los Gatos. It opened for operation in 1855, profiting very little until its closure in 1857. Due to delays with his order for the machinery and his financial troubles caused by the litigation with the New Almaden Quicksilver Mines, the Forbes Mill led to his bankruptcy. The Company of Samuels and Farmer bought the mill in 1862, and it became the Los Gatos Manufacturing Company. The community that grew around this mill—the first real employer in this area—was once named Forbestown. Later, it reverted back to the name Los Gatos.[16]

The other first large commercial mill was the Lick Mill between Alviso and San Jose. These mills, one on the Los Gatos Creek and the other on the Guadalupe River, struggled due to flooding and insufficient water flow. Subsequent mills depended on steam power from artesian wells, a more reliable source of power. All Santa Clara County mills were closed by 1898.

Pacific Manufacturing Company

J. P. Pierce founded the Enterprise Mill in Santa Clara 1874. The mill was reorganized in 1880 as the Pacific Manufacturing Company, with twelve employees, $20,000 worth of capital, $3,000 worth of goods, and $21,000

William A. Wulf

70

980   Pacific Manufacturing Co., Santa Clara, Cal.

William A. Wulf

worth of product. It manufactured coffins, doors, blinds, sashes, and planks. Historian Munro-Fraser noted in 1881 that the Pacific Manufacturing Company was one of the most complete coffin emporiums in the United States. The mill expanded onto the land that was once Cook's Pond, once a recreational center for Santa Clara and San Jose, and one of Father Catalá's sources for willow saplings. After the 1906 earthquake, the mill was running 16 hours a day to supply San Jose with enough building material to reconstruct after the devastation. J. H. Pierce, son of J. P. Pierce, assumed presidency of the company around this time.

In World War I, it began manufacturing airplane parts; and in the late 1920s, it built a new mill and main office on The Alameda to accommodate its growing business. During this time it became one of the largest employers in Santa Clara County.[17]

Eberhard Tannery

When recalling the Eberhard Tannery, life-long resident of San Jose Bill Wulf noted, "P U it smelt bad!" Despite its foul odor, the Eberhard Tannery was an important employer

on The Alameda half a century ago. Before closing in 1953, the tannery provided residents of The Alameda and Santa Clara County with saddles, harnesses, plow tethers, and shoe soles for over a century. In 1849, Louis Wampach owned the tannery, but it may have been in business earlier than that—in 1846, a San Francisco paper advertised "a tannery in Santa Clara" for sale. Wampach sold the tannery to Henry Messing and Isaac Dixon in 1854, and Philip Glein bought the tannery in 1857.

Philip Glein's daughter, Mary, originally attracted Jacob Eberhard to the Santa Clara Tannery. Jacob and Mary first met in Sacramento, where Jacob opened a harness shop after spending four years in the gold fields. Jacob had considerable experience in the harness and saddle making business when he began making trips to the Santa Clara Tannery. Jacob Eberhard was 27 when he finally married Mary on November 1, 1864. Eberhard, a leading industrial pioneer of the time, bought the business two years later. By the 1890s, the tannery produced 29,000 cow hides, 3,000 calf hides, and 100,000 sheep hides per year. Occupying 11 acres by 1915, it was known as one of the largest tanneries in the world. Jacob

and Mary had a son named Oscar Eberhard, the next owner of the company. When Oscar Eberhard was company president, the Eberhard Tannery was reputed to be the oldest tannery on the Pacific Coast and the oldest firm in Santa Clara County. Business peaked in 1924 and 1925, when the tannery employed 100 men and produced 200 hides a day. The tannery employed as many as one in four Santa Clarans at this time, and an especially large number of German immigrants. The tannery's decline can be attributed to the end of the "wild west"

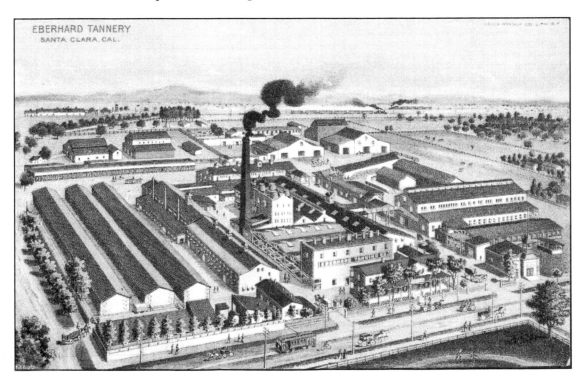

The tall smoke stack toppled in the 1906 earthquake. The old adobe office and the fire house are at the lower right. The three long sheds at the far left stored tanbark.

and the development of the neolite shoe sole. By the thirties there was no longer a high demand for leather. When farmers in the valley stopped plowing with horses and began using tractors, plow tether sales plummeted. The tannery business further declined around 1933 when gypsies started a fire and destroyed the leather sole department.

The tannery closed in the 1950's and was demolished to make way for the ever-expanding Santa Clara University. In 1950, Miss Isabel de Saisset bequeathed the old Metropole Hotel to the Jesuit Order. In 1953, Santa Clara University acquired the Eberhard Tannery by trading its hotel property and a small cash payment. This acquisition enabled the university to expand its campus across Grant Street, past the Ryan Athletic Field. The tannery buildings were razed and additional university buildings were built on the six acres.[18]

The Last Willows

Over time, the willows were all gradually replaced by sycamores, poplars, and elms as the old trees died out. In 1917, there were 13 original willows remaining. In 1932, only three remained. When two of the last three willows began to die in 1932, there was a movement to rescue them. Tree surgeons sealed "ominous cracks" in the trees with cement (though this is an outdated practice that has proved unhelpful to dying trees).[1]

In 1932, the city tree commission began an early beautification movement on The Alameda. They replaced the dead, dying, dangerous, and diseased elms, cottonwoods, willows and black locusts with 2,000 European Sycamores.[2] During this time, the commission removed two willows between McKendrie and University Streets as a safety measure, but they made an effort to rescue the other three

last surviving descendants of Catalá's 1799 willows. The Santa Clara council ordered 15,000 trees to be raised in a city nursery.[3]

Two years later, Rev. James J. Lyons, S. J., president of the Santa Clara University, blessed the three willows, and the Catalá Club of Santa Clara University marked them with bronze plaques. Two of the trees stood in front of 1860 The Alameda and the third tree fronted 1990 The Alameda.[4]

The San Jose Mercury referred to these three last trees as "black willows" (more

This photo was taken in 1933. Father A. D. Spearman captioned it, "An Original Padre Catalá Alameda black native willow." This was the second to last of Catalá's willows. The last willow on The Alameda was an offshoot of one of the original willows. It was in front of 1860 The Alameda, and disappeared mysteriously in 1982.[5]

precisely termed "Goodings black willow." Black willows, or Salix nigra, are only found on the East Coast. The Goodings black willow is California's version of the Salix nigra).

In 1938, city councilman Fred Doerr led a movement to replant trees down the center of The Alameda when the street was torn up to remove the streetcar tracks. The city authorized Engineer M. H. Antonacci to survey the road and determine how they might restore the ancient central parkway. Unfortunately, traffic issues precluded the proposed restoration.

The willow at 1990 The Alameda was the next to disappear. Uprooted for progress's sake in 1961, this willow was removed for a Route 17 freeway onramp.

The story of Catalá's last willow is a mysterious one. The stubby, 15-foot tall tree began to die, but was rejuvenated after being topped. Though not the most attractive tree, residents of The Alameda cherished this historic landmark. The ancient tree firmly clung to its life until its unnatural death at the dawn of October 16, 1982. City officials believe that the tree was removed illegally on this date. The punishment for removing a street tree was $500 or a six-month jail term at that time, so no one ever took responsibility for cutting the tree down.

On October 15, at 2:10 am, a car ran into a lamppost, which fell over and broke a tree-branch. The police officer investigating the accident ordered a pickup truck to clean up the debris. Soon afterward, the last willow vanished. Frank Garcia, superintendent in the San Jose Department of Neighborhood Maintenance, claimed that none of his crews had cut it down. Both PG&E, which had crews working in the area, and Caltrans claimed to know nothing about the missing tree. "It's still a mystery…as to who cut the tree down, cleaned up the debris, put up the barricade, and then put the city's mark on the stump," Garcia said. The culprit marked the stump with a symbol used by the city maintenance crews to indicate tree removal. A city official explained, "some people know our symbols and we are finding trees illegally cut down by private individuals who then mark the tree with city's mark for stump removal. This tree was definitely not on our list." The tree's historical plaque mysteriously vanished as well, allegedly some time before the tree vanished.[6]

The trees that exist today probably provide as much shade and aesthetic appeal as their willow predecessors. The new trees signify progress and the march of time. Many willows were sacrificed to make way for the constant change that has always been a part of the history of this boulevard. This new era, the era of the sycamores, beckons The Alameda into the future and promises new successes and achievements.

In the past couple of years there has been an explosion of development along The Alameda. The Avalon Apartments, Long's Drugs, and Peet's are some recent additions. Farmers Markets thrive on The Alameda as the state fairs once did in 1890 in The Agricultural Park. One can still visit Schurra's and Greenlee's Bakery, the two oldest businesses on the street. It is important to recognize these companies as historical landmarks and remember the historically important places along the street. This is why a walking tour of The Alameda has been included in this history—to explain the meaning behind the historic buildings and locations.

Become a part of the history of The Alameda. Take a stroll down the street and see the history come alive in the Walking Tour of The Alameda!

THE ALAMEDA

The Beautiful Way

Excerpt from *An Arboreal Song of the Alameda, the Beautiful Way,* by Mary H. Field, 1878

"The friar's years went onward gliding,
But the beauteous Vision did ne'er depart,
Like an angel presence still abiding,
It cheered forever that faithful heart,
And those who loved him and shared his going
To care for the willows day by day,
Would hear him say as he watched their growing,
'My blessed Vision! My Beautiful Way!'

Till the Pueblos rang with the grateful praising
Of the road where the pleasant shadows lay,
And the people named it in happy phrasing
'The Alameda!'—The Beautiful Way!

The Mission Fathers are gone,—
Peace to the saintly dead!
Its walls have crumbled down,
And the Neophytes are all fled.

I too am my end anear,
And the sere leaved shook anew,
Falling are my brothers dear,—
But the Friar's Vision was true!

The Rune of Tree was done,
But my thoughts still sang to me,
As leaves go whispering on
Though the breeze of the morn doth flee.

Gone are the fathers all!
In the chapel's crypt they lie,
Where no tender rain may fall,
Or gleam from our sunny sky.

No sculptured marble doth show
Each old historic name;
No blazoned window doth glow
With record of their fame,

But their living monument stands to-day
In The Alameda—The Beautiful Way!"

What's In a Name?

Stockton Avenue

Commodore Robert F. Stockton arrived in California during the Mexican-American War as the commander of the Pacific squadron. After serving as the military governor of California, he returned to the East Coast in 1847. He never revisited his land in California, but managed it from New Jersey. In the 1850s he served as the Governor of New Jersey. In 1850, he ordered the Alameda Gardens Subdivision (on The Alameda) to be mapped, and he imported 10 to 13 houses from the east coast for this development.

Sunol Street

Don Antonio Maria Suñol, the first postmaster and well-educated settler of San Jose purchased Los Coches Ranch from the Indian, Roberto, in 1847. His adobe, built by Roberto in 1839, remains on Lincoln Avenue, now known as Lauraville.

Rhodes Court

Judge Augustus L. Rhodes owned the property next to this street and lived in a house at that was imported from the east coast.

Morrison Avenue

In about 1866, Andrew L. Morrison moved into a house on The Alameda that was imported from the east coast. Legend has it that Morrison was deaf, but this did not stop him from collecting tolls at Shartzer's tollgate near Julian Street. James H. Peirce, the owner of the Pacific Manufacturing Company, executed the property and established the Morrison Subdivision around what is now Morrison Avenue.

Race Street

Until the turn of the century, a racetrack ran adjacent to Race Street. On this track, located in the Agricultural Park, Stanford raced his horses and Barney Oldfield broke the world's auto speed record, reaching 60 miles per hour in 1903.

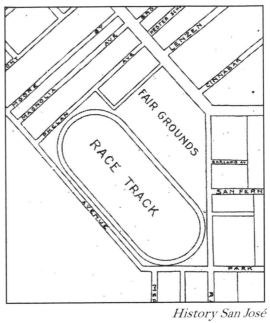

History San José

West Julian Street

The part of this street that connects to The Alameda used to be an extension of Cinnabar Street, a name inspired by the New Almaden Quicksilver Mines. During the early 1800s, many residents around The Alameda invested in these mines. Cinnabar is the rock where mercury is found. Before it was officially Cinnabar Street, William Campbell referred to the street as "St. Julian" in an 1848 map.

Hanchett Avenue

Lewis E. Hanchett developed the Hanchett Residence Park, one of San Jose's first "streetcar suburbs." Hanchett built a car line from The Alameda to Park Avenue and Race Street via Martin and Tillman Avenues. By

1907, Hanchett had joined Bishop as a "giant of San Jose transit," according to historian Clyde Arbuckle.

Lenzen Avenue

The esteemed architect Theodore Lenzen was born in Prussia in 1833. Throughout his career he designed up to 600 buildings, including the Fredericksburg Brewery. Lenzen subdivided the land around Lenzen Avenue.

Pershing Avenue

General John Joseph Pershing led the American Expeditionary Force in World War I.

Magnolia Avenue

Judge John Henley Moore came to San Jose in 1849 and purchased 14 acres east of Magnolia Avenue on The Alameda. His square colonial home was known for its garden of redwoods, magnolias, and lilacs. Magnolia Avenue was named for these magnolias. In 1946, The Alameda was home to the two largest magnolia trees in the state of California. These magnolia trees were located east of the bend at Race Street, at 1061 The Alameda.

Singletary Avenue

The early pioneer Emory C. Singletary, who lived on Stockton Avenue, was one of the well-to-do agriculturists of Santa Clara County. At one time he was one of the largest landholders in the state, holding title to over 35 thousand acres. He was the first vice president of the First National Bank of San Jose and was one of the directors of the State Agricultural Society for a number of years. The Singletary family owned land between Fremont and Singletary Avenue, and Emory Singletary's descendants lived there.

Fremont Street

John Charles Fremont was one of the four major generals appointed by President Lincoln during the Civil War. As one of California's first senators, Fremont was a key player in the Bear Flag Revolt.

Schiele Avenue

Charles M. Schiele, a Prussian immigrant, took over operation of the Pacific Hotel in 1880. According to historian Donald O. Demers, "under Schiele's proprietorship the Pacific Hotel became one of the most popular stopping places in SJ." The hotel was removed in 1907 due to the earthquake, but a replica now stands in Kelley Park. Schiele purchased 15 acres between The Alameda and Stockton Avenue for $75,000 and developed a subdivision around Schiele Avenue.

Villa Avenue

The Alameda Villa Tract surrounded this street in 1892.

Randol Avenue

James B. Randol owned 218 acres surrounding Randol Avenue, called the Randol Addition. J. B. Randol arrived from New York in 1870 as the newly appointed general manager of the Quicksilver Mines.

Taylor Street

This street was originally Polhemus Street, named for Charles B. Polhemus. The C. B. Polhemus family lived at the southwest corner of Taylor Street and Stockton Avenue. Their estate was named the "Pendennis." This house was shipped to California in hardwood sections from Massachusetts. This house burned to the ground in 1914.

Naglee Avenue

General Henry C. Naglee helped found the first banking house in San Francisco. He owned a portion of Los Coches Ranch, one of the two ranches that lined The Alameda in its early days. The General's vineyard and winery is now Naglee Park.

University Avenue

The University of the Pacific occupied what is now the Bellarmine Campus between 1866 and 1925. The University relocated to Stockton, but the name of this street remains.

Asbury, Emory, McKendrie, and Hedding Streets

The University of the Pacific, a Methodist institution, named these streets after Methodist Bishops when they subdivided College Park in 1866.

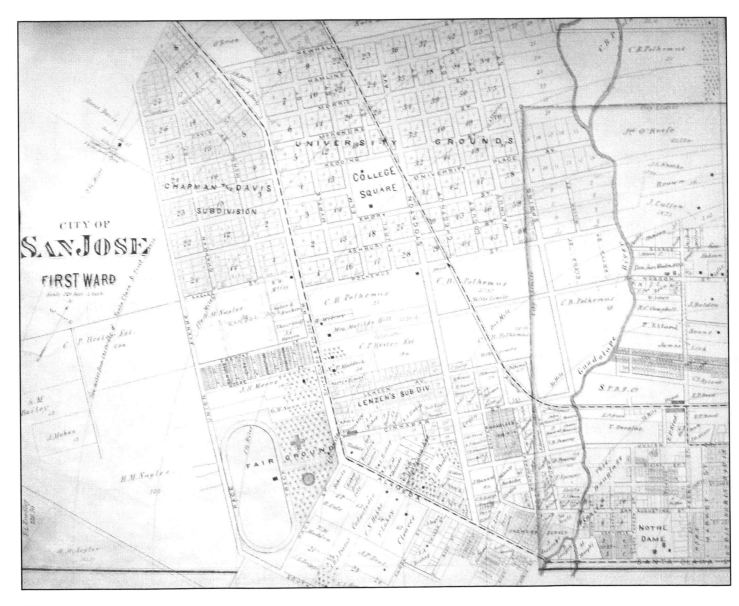

William A. Wulf

Plaque Sites:

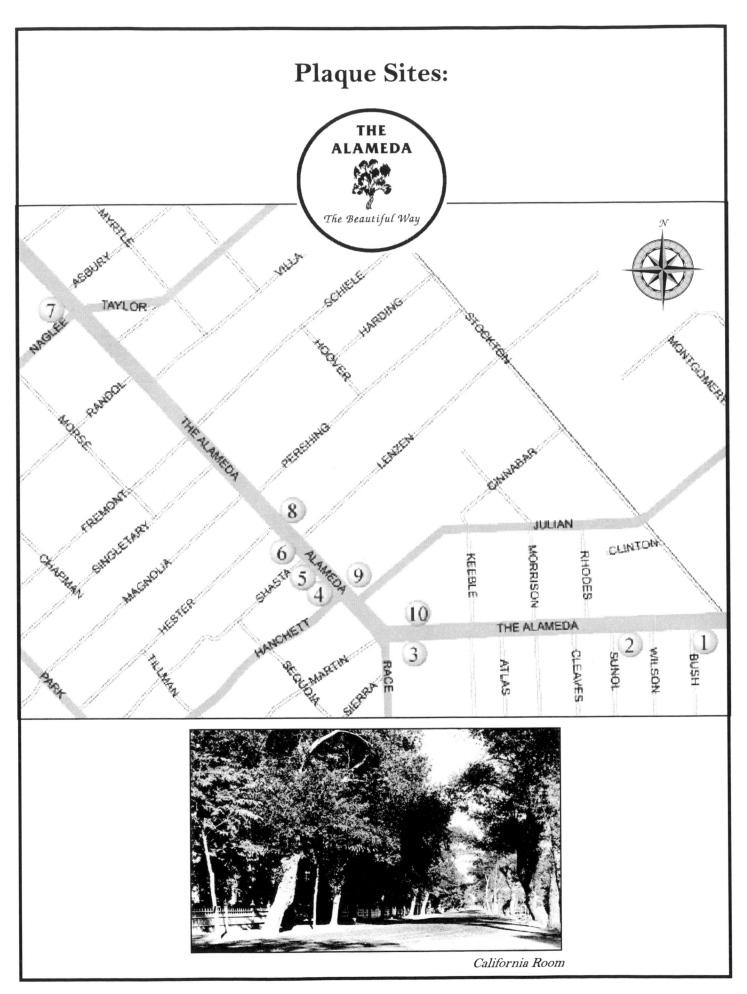

THE
ALAMEDA

The Beautiful Way

California Room

WALKING TOUR OF THE ALAMEDA

PLAQUE 1

PLANT 51--OUR TOUR BEGINS WITH THE CALPAK DISTRICT MANAGER'S OFFICE.
734 The Alameda

History San José

The District Manager operated seven California Fruit Packers Association (Calpak) plants from this red brick office building between 1930 and 1990. The cannery itself was located behind this office, covering almost a whole city block. Only three former Calpak cannery sites remain. Calpak was the first canner to nationally advertise and distribute its products under the single brand name, "Del Monte."

PACIFIC WINE COMPANY'S BUILDINGS, SAN JOSE, CAL.

California Room

The Griffin & Skelley Co. Dried Fruit Packers originally built this plant in 1914. Prior to the construction of this cannery, the Pacific Wine Company made wine at this location.

This railroad crossing "shanty" was located on the former South Pacific Coast Railroad (later bought by the Southern Pacific Railroad), on the north side of The Alameda. When the train came, the flagman would stop traffic with a flag (where the overpass is now). Originally, this building served as one of two ticket booths built for the Southern Pacific Railroad's display at the 1895 Mid-winter Fair, in San Francisco. This photo was taken around 1910, and the two flagman shanties survived until the 1920's. The other one was located at the First Street crossing.

As you look across The Alameda toward the intersection of Stockton, there used to be a gas station and later, a drive-in restaurant at the corner. In this picture, taken between 1935 and 1938, the electric streetcar is headed downtown, towards the Southern Pacific Railway underpass, the replacement for the flagman's shanty.

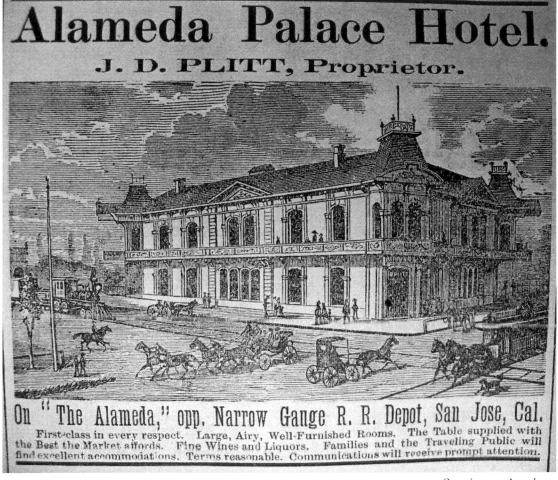

Alameda Palace Hotel.
J. D. PLITT, Proprietor.

On "The Alameda," opp. Narrow Gauge R. R. Depot, San Jose, Cal.

First-class in every respect. Large, Airy, Well-Furnished Rooms. The Table supplied with the Best the Market affords. Fine Wines and Liquors. Families and the Traveling Public will find excellent accommodations. Terms reasonable. Communications will receive prompt attention.

Sourisseau Academy

The Alameda Palace Hotel used to stand across from the West San Jose Depot, the corner of White Street and The Alameda. By 1905, it was referred to as the "notorious Palace hotel" for various reasons. The second floor of this hotel can still be seen at 633 Morse Street, where it serves as a second floor of a residential home.

CONTINUE WEST
CROSS BUSH STREET

754 The Alameda
Built in 1922, a building at this location served as the Western Pacific Railroad freight depot until 1967. It was later an "Archer's Den." Today, the Avalon at Cahill Park Apartments are situated at this location.

CROSS WILSON AVENUE
CROSS SUNOL STREET

William A. Wulf

808 The Alameda

Note the 15-foot figure in front of Babe's Muffler Service. "Babe" has been holding this muffler since 1954. Roland "Babe" Royer established Babe's muffler service in 1953 at 955 The Alameda, and the company moved to 808 The Alameda the following year. In 1954, a model of Paul Bunyan holding an ax caught Royer's eye when he was at a trade show. It inspired him to use Paul Bunyan as a roadside advertising gimmick. Royer turned Paul Bunyan into "Babe," the first of many Babes that would advertise for Royer's shops throughout northern California.

PLAQUE 2
SCHURRA'S.
848 The Alameda

Take note of The Alameda's most historic candy shop, which had its start in 1912. Alphonse and Anna Schurra emigrated from France with their son Justin. Their second son, Albert, was born in Washington on their way to California. While Anna and Alphonse settled on a farm in Sunnyvale, the boys pursued candy making. Albert opened a store in Modesto before he opened shop on The Alameda in 1938. Schurra's occupied the 125-year-old brick building at the corner of The Alameda and Sunol for four decades. At the new Schurra's location next-door, Brian Mundy continues to use original Schurra recipes.

CONTINUE WEST
CROSS SUNOL STREET
CROSS CLEAVES STREET

The current location of the Billy DeFrank LGBT Community Center was a French restaurant from 1929 to 1939, and later, an Arthur Murray Dance Studio.

William A. Wulf

965 The Alameda

Look across the street at the ivy-covered building, shown in the picture on the previous page. This building was the home of the Leland Cerruti Packard Dealership in San Jose. It had stunning architectural features in the Spanish Revival style, including ornate outdoor hanging lamps, some of which are still visible today. Many of the ornate features have been removed, but the front showroom is in nearly original condition. New Packards (ca. 1929) are displayed in the showroom window. These were mid-price range cars during that time. Also note the reflection in the window. Under close inspection, one will see a reflection of the building across the street, next to Savin's. This was a gas station advertising Standard Oil Products. Around this time, 27% of all businesses east of Magnolia Avenue were oriented to automobiles sales and service.

CROSS SOUTH MORRISON AVENUE
CROSS ATLAS AVENUE

1040 The Alameda

Visualize a 1930s Miniature Golf Course, pictured below, in the place of Enterprise Rent-a-Car. Behind the Victorian house next-door stood Power's Urn Shop.

History San José

CONTINUE WEST
CROSS SOUTH KEEBLE AVENUE

1041 The Alameda

As you look across The Alameda, this is the view you would have seen of TraveLodge in the 1950s:

63 Units, indiv. A.C., D.D. Phones, T. V. (some color) Heated Pool, some queen size beds, 4 Restaurants within a block. Centrally located between S.J.S. College and University of Santa Clara.

History San José

PLAQUE 3
THE AUDITORIUM ROLLER RINK.
1064 The Alameda

You have now arrived at one of the architectural jewels of The Alameda. This ornate building was the Auditorium Roller Rink from 1927 to 1974. You can still see the smooth wood floors if you are invited into "Art Works" which currently occupies the rear of the building. J. E. Cassidy owned the rink until Robert B. Roll took over management in 1949. Through the years, many champion skaters practiced here. Also known as Roll-Ameda, the rink was a popular weekend attraction for children who lived near The Alameda especially in the pre-war years. Roll recalled that in the rink's early years, "Girls coming in with skating skirts would have to kneel on the floor. We'd put one of those little Coke bottles down there and if there was any space at all between the hem of the skirt and the top of the bottle then they didn't skate." Connie Trevino, a long-time resident of The Alameda, remembers that it cost about 35 cents to rent skates there, and notes, "we would dance with all the sailors who would go there during the war."

CONTINUE WEST
CROSS RACE STREET AND MARTIN AVENUE

1205 The Alameda
You are now standing at the intersection of Martin Avenue and The Alameda. In 1911, the house at this corner belonged to August Marten. Contrary to popular belief, Martin Avenue was not named after August Marten. What is now Togo's, Mission Pipe Shop, and Pasta Pomodoro, used to be a popular hangout in the 1940s—Tiny's Drive In. Tiny's replaced the Marten house in 1941.

William A. Wulf

Before Tiny's in the 1940s and before any house was built as part of the Hanchett Subdivision, the entrance to the Agricultural Park stood at this location. The Agricultural Park encompassed 76 acres of land bordered by Race Street, The Alameda, Magnolia Avenue and Park Avenue. The Santa Clara Valley Agricultural Society began to have state fairs in 1856, but finally bought this park in 1859. The Agricultural Society's fundraising committee sold subscriptions and raised $14,464.55 in just two weeks. The Society paid General Naglee $6,000 for the 76-acre parcel. This allowed the society to use the remaining funds to improve the park. This park served as a recreational facility for over 40 years. Livestock fairs, circuses, and dances made this one of the most popular San Jose parks. Leland Stanford

Leonard McKay

raced his prize horses, Palo Alto and Occident, in the famous racing track located there. After returning from his trip around the world in 1879, President Grant visited The Agricultural Park to watch Occident race against the clock. In 1905, the "father of basic flying" and inventor of the cambered wing, John J. Montgomery, gave some of the

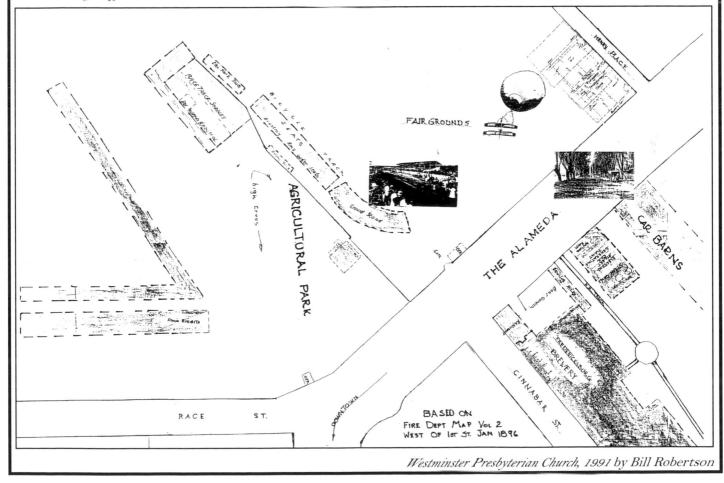

Westminster Presbyterian Church, 1991 by Bill Robertson

first public flight demonstrations of a heavier than air high-air glider in the Agricultural Park.

CONTINUE NORTHWEST
CROSS HANCHETT AVENUE

PLAQUE 4
FRANCO'S SUPER MARKET
1341-1345 The Alameda

The old and highly decorated building that the Teak House and Commuknity occupy was built as the Hester Public Market in 1925. In 1944, Joey Franco opened a Franco's Super Market in this building. The store on The Alameda was one of the first grocery stores in his ten-store chain.

CONTINUE TOWARD THE WESTMINISTER PRESBYTERIAN CHURCH.

PLAQUE 5
WESTMINSTER PRESBYTERIAN CHURCH.
1341-1345 The Alameda

This land also used to be part of the Agricultural Park. The Westminster Presbyterian Church traces roots to the first Protestant church in San Jose. Reverend John Douglas organized the Independent Presbyterian Church with a band of six Christian pioneer families on October 7, 1849, and a church was built on North Second Street. This original church was rebuilt in 1890 as the Second Presbyterian Church.

The congregation had outgrown the Church by 1925. The Westminster Church was built to accommodate the growing congregation in 1926. You can still see stained-glass windows from the original Second Presbyterian Church incorporated in the construction of the Westminster Church.

Clyde Arbuckle

The Second Presbyterian Church on North Second Street.

CONTINUE NORTHWEST
CROSS SHASTA AVENUE

1401 The Alameda

In 1896, Kane, Moulton & Co. Real Estate Agents stood at the current location of Realty World.

History San José

PLAQUE 6
THE HESTER THEATER.
1433 The Alameda

The Hester Theater, renamed the Towne theater in 1949, was the first neighborhood theater in San Jose. In 1930 it was the first theater in San Jose to install a sound system to accommodate the "talkies." On May 1, 1930, the Mercury Herald announced, "Hester Theater opens with Talking Pictures, talking as you've never heard them talk before!" Mason Shaw took over the Towne Theater in 1955. After Mason Shaw played a controversial Danish film in 1969, *I Am Curious Yellow*, the theater was closed down. When a court decision allowed such films to be shown, a wave of adult movies spread throughout the valley. Camera Cinemas, led by James Zuur, renovated the Towne, adding two smaller theaters in the 1980s. Since then, it has specialized in showing foreign films. Currently, it is the home of the India Movie Center, which shows first run movies from India.

Jack Douglas

BANK OF ITALY
1445 The Alameda

At the Hester Avenue intersection, note the Spanish Colonial Revival style of the Bank of Italy building. A.P. Giannini began the Bank of Italy in San Francisco in 1904. As one of the first local branches of the Bank of Italy, the Hester branch was constructed in 1926, the same year as the 13-story Bank of Italy building on the corner of Santa Clara and First Street. Prestigious architect H. A. Minton designed both. In 1930 the Bank of Italy became Bank of America.

CONTINUE NORTHWEST
CROSS HESTER AVENUE

1457 The Alameda
At the current location of the Shell Gas Station, Justin Schurra opened a confectionary in 1925. In 1933, Justin moved his candy store to Sunnyvale, near the old theater on Murphy Avenue. Albert Schurra, his brother, brought Schurra's Candy back to The Alameda in 1938.

CONTINUE NORTHWEST
CROSS MAGNOLIA AVENUE

AS YOU CROSS SINGLETARY AVENUE, NOTE THE HESTER GATES. This elegant brick entrance was built in 1904 when the Hester Park housing development began.

CONTINUE NORTHWEST
CROSS FREMONT STREET
CROSS RANDOL AVENUE
CROSS NAGLEE AVENUE

PLAQUE 7
THE YMCA AND HART MANSION.
1717 The Alameda

In 1920, Alexander J. Hart, president of L. Hart & Son department store, built a home at this location for $125,000. As a gift to his wife Nettie, it was patterned after the Petit Trianon of Versailles. In this house, the Harts received an ominous 1933 phone call. Jack Holmes and Thomas H. Thurmond kidnapped 22-year-old Brooke Hart, A. J. Hart's son, in the parking lot of the department store. After kidnapping Brooke, they threw him over the San Mateo bridge and decided a week later to call the Hart home demanding $40,000. The call was traced and the two criminals were arrested. San Jose residents were so infuriated by this brutal and calloused murder that a mob broke into the jail and the two kidnappers were lynched in St. James Park.

The YMCA purchased this property in 1953. The Hart mansion was replaced by basketball courts, racquetball courts, work-out rooms, and a pool, but a sundial that was originally part of the landscaping of the Hart mansion can still be seen in the courtyard behind the YMCA building.

Alex Hart, Jr.

CROSS THE ALAMEDA
CROSS TAYLOR STREET
CONTINUE SOUTHEAST

CALPAK PLAQUE (1951)

DAWSON RESIDENCE.

Corner of Taylor Street and The Alameda

FRUIT PACKING, SAN JOSE, CALIFORNIA   7111

The San Jose canning industry originated on The Alameda in a residence at this location. Farmers needed a way to exploit new markets with their expanding fruit and vegetable crops. Dr. James M. Dawson met this need by developing a way to preserve the fruit grown here in the "Valley of Heart's Delight." During the summer of 1871, Dr. James M. Dawson and his family canned 350 cases of fruit in a 12x16 woodshed behind their home. This was the birthplace of canned food production in the Valley, which reached its peak in the 1940s. At this time, Santa Clara County produced 90 percent of California's canned food.

CONTINUE SOUTHEAST
CROSS VILLA AVENUE
CROSS SCHIELE AVENUE
CROSS PERSHING AVENUE

PLAQUE 8

1460 The Alameda

You are now in front of Hester School, currently housing the Downtown College Preparatory. Hester School has occupied this location for over a century. Hester School opened in the 1860s and was named for the Judge Craven P. Hester, one of the first residents on The Alameda.

History San José

NOTE THE HESTER PEDESTRIAN TUNNEL. The Hester Pedestrian Subway was designed by W. L. Popp and built in 1928 in memory of two students of Hester School. Students Virginia A. Frazer and Charles Loring Sykes were killed by speeding automobiles on The Alameda. This tunnel was designed to provide school children with a safe way to cross the street.

CONTINUE SOUTHEAST
CROSS LENZEN AVENUE

PLAQUE 9
FREDERICKSBURG BREWERY.
1338 The Alameda

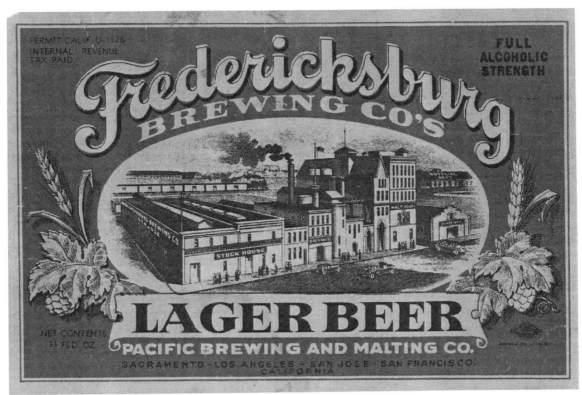

William A. Wulf

Beer was brewed for over 110 years at the current site of the Avalon on The Alameda Apartments. In 1869, Gottfried Frederick Krahenberg, a German tavern keeper, set up a brewery in a small brick shanty at this location. Theodore Lenzen designed a massive brick brew and malt house to replace the shanty in 1872. The Fredericksburg Brewery quickly became one of the largest breweries in Santa Clara Valley. Initially, the brewery produced 4,000 to 5,000 barrels of beer per year, and 53,000 barrels per year by 1888. The Fredericksburg's advertisement was simple: "It is the best." Even after a 1902 fire destroyed the malt house, it was still "the biggest pile of bricks in town." The castle-like turrets of the Brewery fell during the earthquake of 1906. *California Today* once noted that it "withstood the earthquake of 1906 but could not survive Prohibition." After 1918, it was closed. Until the prohibition laws were repealed in 1933, James A Talbot tried to operate the brewery, producing "near beer," only to lose money. The Pacific Brewing and Malting Company purchased it in 1936. The Fredericksburg label lasted until 1939, when it was relabeled Wieland's Beer.

In 1952, the Falstaff Brewing Corporation bought the Pacific Brewing and Malting Company. Falstaff produced six million cases each year on The Alameda, but unfortunately for The Alameda, this was not enough to meet demand. Operations were consolidated in San Francisco, where the company was able to produce twenty million cases a year. The San Jose plant was torn down in 1980.

Hiram Schartzer's tollgate stood at West Julian and The Alameda in the 1860s. In 1862, Hiram Shartzer began the Alameda Turnpike Company, making The Alameda one of the earliest toll roads in California. The tollgate charged 10 cents for single buggies, 25 cents for teams, and $1 for stages.

CONTINUE EAST
CROSS WEST JULIAN STREET

1280 The Alameda
Note the vibrant mural on the side of Andy's Pet Shop and its neon parrot sign. Alameda residents have purchased their pets at Andy's since 1950. Before Andy's, this building served as a Highway Patrol office for many years. The patrol car garages in the rear of this building can still be seen from West Julian Street.

PLAQUE 10
GREENLEE'S.

Frank Mitchell Greenlee and Harriett J. Greenlee moved to San Jose in 1925 with their son Emmett Greenlee. Frank constructed this building on The Alameda in the 1920's and opened his bakery in 1929. Emmett operated the bakery until he sold it to Rosalinda and Norbert Geldner in 1981. Almost eighty years since its beginning, Greenlee's bakery continues to entice the passerby with its aromatic sticky-cinnamon loaves.

Greenlee's

THE END

Photo by Rex Kuehner

California Room

William A. Wulf

HANCHETT RESIDENCE PARK
Walking History Tour

Cassandra Ravenscroft

Hanchett Residence Park tract, as it was originally called, includes Mariposa, Yosemite, Sierra, Martin, Sequoia, Hanchett (Busch Avenue until 1918 when residents petitioned county supervisors), Shasta, and Tillman Avenues, between Park Avenue and The Alameda. Race Street, another subdivision boundary, was named for the horseracing track that was located along this street where Leland Stanford raced his steeds.

This subdivision originally was the site the 76-acre county *Agricultural Park*, a popular park and fairgrounds for over 40 years. It included a horseracing track, bicycle velodrome, baseball fields, picnic grounds and a variety of other facilities. It was also the home to over 2,600 forest and ornamental trees. Traveling circuses raised their big tops and balloonists used the area as a launching pad. Some of the state's most famous racehorses and bike riders had set records on its tracks. President Grant had also visited the Park in 1879. And, in 1903 the 9th Cavalry – an African-American troop commonly known as the Buffalo Soldiers –even camped here en route to patrol duties in Yosemite and Sequoia National Parks.

During the depression years of the 1890's, the park could no longer meet its expenses, and was thus sold in 1901 to Lewis Hanchett's, Peninsula Land and Development Co. In 1905 Hanchett personally acquired the land; however, he was unsure as to what he wanted to do with it. *"…leave it a park and make improvements, or something else"*. The something else prevailed, and the area was subdivided into one of San Jose's most affluent and desirable neighborhoods. The cover of the original sales brochure proudly stated " *We challenge comparison with any subdivision offered anyplace on the Peninsula, as far as quality of the improvements and location of tract are concerned"*. The tract was surveyed in June 1906 and recorded the following December. It was not until April 7, 1908 that county supervisors voted to accept the streets in the park as public roads.

Lot prices ranged from $450 up. Terms: $25 down and $10 per month per lot. No lower offers were entertained, as protection to those who bought first. To the contrary, prices were advanced from time to time--when 50% of lots were sold.

Residents purchased individual lots in Hanchett Park, hired their own architects and builders, so many of the homes were custom built within the guidelines allowed by Hanchett. Most homes were built between 1915 and 1930, many in the *Craftsman bungalow, Mission,* and *Spanish Eclectic* style. A few *Prairie style* homes are scattered in the neighborhood as well. The Victorians in the neighborhood pre-date the development of Hanchett Park subdivision.

Hanchett Park tract amenities included: electric streetlights on ornamental poles, a streetcar branch, flush toilets, and a state-of-the-art septic tank sewer system. Sewer pipes were large and laid so well, that the system was capable of meeting the demands of a population 3x as large. In its time, it was the only subdivision ever placed on the market in California with a modern septic sewer system and flush tanks. To maintain its residential exclusivity, stores, saloons, laundries, wood yards, and other places of business were not permitted in the tract area.

It also offered the best streets, curbs, and sidewalks that money could buy. Principal streets were 80' wide, not 60' as standard. The area was also higher and drier than any other subdivision around San Jose, and it was claimed that it has never been known to have water standing upon it, thus insuring every advantage of a healthful location.

Hanchett hired John McLaren, the superintendent and designer of Golden Gate Park to design the streetscape. McLaren laid out the curving streets and carefully placed utility poles in the backyards to avoid sidewalk clutter. He placed granite monuments at the Tillman and Sequoia intersections at Martin and chose species of tree for each street. Trees were to be placed 20 feet apart on each side of every street in the tract.

Sequoia—Cork Oak	Martin--Palm
Yosemite—Calif. Black Walnut	Hanchett & Tillman--Black Locust
Sierra--Chestnut	Shasta & Mariposa--Sycamore

While the early advertising brochures for Hanchett Residence Park show a drawing of a grand mansion proposed to be built for Lewis Hanchett in the park, this particular home does not exist in the neighborhood, and we have not been able to find any listings for Hanchetts residing in the park in the old City Directories.

Lewis Hanchett was an ambitious, wise investor. He was only 33 years old when he purchased the San Jose and Santa Clara electric railway in partnership with John Martin (namesake for Martin Ave.), co-founder of PG&E. He became the force behind San Jose's transit system. Due to the many technological improvements he made in the industry, fruit and other produce could be shipped to San Jose from outlying areas, thus causing a stronger economy overall in the area.

Hanchett Park has been designated a Historic Conservation Area by the City of San Jose, in an effort to preserve its beauty and character.

RESIDENCES of HANCHETT PARK

CRAFTSMAN ARCHITECTURE

Bungalow style was influenced by Japanese & Swiss chalet architecture. Instead of Gingerbread, natural rocks and stone, locally fired bricks and tiles, local woods, simple varge boards and geometric windows.

- Wide overhanging eaves
- Columned front porches for outdoor living – doors open directly into living room.
- Always a fireplace – FLW the hearth is the Heart of the Home
- Shed roof
- Dormer windows on side
- Combination wood and stucco
- Built ins
- Natural materials, of the earth, local region

#1: **1167& 77 Hanchett** – Here we have two early examples of Craftsman bungalows. We want to point out a few features, and there will be many more throughout the tour. The Arts and Crafts movement began in the late 1800s in England, a reaction to fussiness and excess of the Victorian era, but also a reaction to the changes wrought by the Industrial era.

This was a return to simplicity, to handicraft, bringing style to all people regarding of social stature. Over time, this movement spread through the United States, through the advertising of the railroad companies and land developers encouraging families to move west and in the house plans and kits available for sale through the Sears & Roebuck catalog.

COLONIAL REVIVAL ARCHITECTURE

- Miniature temple fronts
- Windows in bands
- French doors
- Classical details – your little piece of Monticello

#2: 1130 Hanchett, we have a Colonial Revival influenced home built in 1921 for Frank Marten. The garage/coachmen's house behind was built earlier as part of the Marten family compound.

Both 1150 and 1168 Hanchett are typical Colonial Revival bungalows that can be seen throughout the neighborhood.

SPANISH ECLECTIC or MISSION ARCHITECTURE

- So named because most houses exhibit details from nearly every era of Spanish, Moorish, and Missionary architectural history
- Tile Roofs
- Stucco Exteriors with elaborate stucco relief work
- Highly stylized spiral columns on facade
- Arched or one large feature window
- Round arches recall a mission cloister
- Sometimes Moorish towers or domes
- Simple interiors, tile accents, some art glass
- Patios

#3: 310 Sequoia Ave (at Hanchett)— In 1923 Ralph Wyckoff, architect of the Downtown Post Office, built this Spanish Eclectic for his residence. He imported fireplace tiles from Spain, and the present residents have found boxes addressed to Wyckoff in the basement.

FARLEY GRANGER:

According to a former resident, the home at 1185 Hanchett was the boyhood home of actor Farley Granger, who is known best from the Hitchcock film "Strangers on a Train."

PRAIRIE ARCHITECTURE

- Truly indigenous American style
- Frank Lloyd Wright – inspired by linear style of Japanese prints he collected and the horizontal lines of the Midwestern Prairie
- Almost all SJ designs are Frank Delos Wolfe
- Low pitched or flat roofs, overhanging eaves
- Massive rectangular piers of masonry with broad flat chimneys
- Rows of casement windows
- Decorative friezes or door surrounds
- Built in furnishings and flowing interiors

#4: 1225 Hanchett Across Sequoia, we come to one of the tracts most "modern" homes with its sunken gardens. This Prairie style home was built prior to 1915 for Charles Mockbee, proprietor of the Gold Nugget Butter Company. It soon sold to Louis Normandin, carriage & auto works, located on The Alameda. The company began as a buggy manufacturer, moved into car building, and today continues as Normandin Chrysler-Plymouth. Lon Normandin, grandson of Louis, remembers playing in the sunken garden as a child. The magnolia tree in the garden is protected as a heritage tree of the city.

#5: 1235 Hanchett – Tudor style bungalow
1257 & 1265 Hanchett – Classic Craftsman bungalows
1294 Hanchett – With paired gables and symmetrical design, this house appears to mirror itself.

#6: 310 Tillman (at Hanchett) was designed and built by Andrew P. Hill Jr. for Frank Hayes, a stockman. Hill was the son of the artist for whom the San Jose high school is named and helped found the Sempervirens Fund and preserve Big Basin State Park. Hill Junior was a talented architect who left San Jose early in his career to become the State Architect. As such, he oversaw the design of many of the school buildings built during California's early growth years and left his Spanish eclectic style on many of them.

#7: 1305 Martin (at Tillman), the residence of Edwin R. and Nina Croft, built in 1911. Charles McKenzie was the architect. In 1915, Nina served as secretary of the Santa Clara County Humane Society. This classic Arts & Crafts home features deep porches, outdoor living rooms and traditional accents such as river rock porch pillars, stucco and wood finish.

GETTING AROUND: Here at the corner of Martin and Tillman, residents could catch the Hanchett Park Streetcar line. The Park was within easy walking distance from the center of SJ, it had streetcar line (2 modern gauge electric car lines) running through the neighborhood from the Alameda. Residents could hop the trolley cars, which ran on Martin, Tillman, and Sequoia Avenues via the Alameda, and to Park Ave. and Race Street, making it only 5 minutes from downtown SJ, and 10 minutes from Santa Clara.

#8: 1288 Martin c. 1922 The only Tudor home on the block. As is the case with most, this Tudor Reveal bears little resemblance to its 16th Century namesake. Steep pitched gable roof, arched entry door, casement windows. Undocumented, but may have been the residence of Phil Hammer, as a boy

#9: Hanchett Park Bungalow Row 1257,1249,1241,1233,1225 Martin: In 1978 the Historic American Building Survey team from Washington D.C. studied, photographed, and drew elevations of these homes which are kept on file at the Library of Congress. Designed by Frank Delos Wolfe and Charles McKenzie, Architects. Wolfe and McKenzie, together and separately, designed many of the homes in the subdivision. Wolfe was one of San Jose's most prolific architects, designing more than 300 buildings in the area during his career, including about 60 homes in the Naglee Park neighborhood east of San Jose State. His early work is classic Craftsman.

1257 Martin. Built in 1910 for Emory G. Singletary of Singletary Brothers, Stocks, Bonds & Loans. Singletary Ave. is named for this family, and the Singletary Mansion remains as office space at the corner of the Alameda and Singletary. Another Singletary had a home built in the first block of Martin Ave., but it is now the parking lot for the commercial businesses.

1249 Martin. Built in 1910 for William H. Gavin. Highly stylized off-center shed dormer, classic entry system, typical Craftsman columns.

1241 Martin. Built in 1910 for M.S. Gibson by Lynn Wolfe, son of famous architect Frank Wolfe. Unique double purlins with verge board held between.

1233 Martin. Built between 1911 and 1912 for Margaret Roberts, a widow.

1225 Martin. Built in 1910 for C.W. Dore, a downtown pharmacist and drugstore owner. Wolfe and McKenzie, architects.

ROBERT FOWLER: San Jose's famous aviation pioneer, Robert Fowler also lived at **1232 Martin.** He learned to fly with Orville Wright in 1911 and was the first man to fly from the west coast to the east.

#10: 1232-34 Martin. Built in 1913. Residence of J.F. Marten, the son of A.H. Marten & Son, Flour, Feed & Grain. A. H. Lived on the Alameda.

#11: 225 Sequoia c. 1924 Believed to be built for C.C. Pomeroy, of Pomeroy & Sons, clothing for men and boys in downtown SJ.

      This Spanish Eclectic house was also designed by Andrew Hill Jr., son of famed SJ artist Andrew Hill, and is an even more impressive example of his work. Note the thick walled adobe-like feeling of the home's construction, the arched detail above windows and some matching arched windows, and the tile accents. The tiles are believed to be the product of S & S – or Solon tiles, the premier tilemaker in San Jose, whose work can be seen on Westminster Church, Old Hoover School, the fountain in the Rose Garden, and the Rosicrucian Museum. Many homes in the neighborhood feature tile accents on the fireplaces or tile fireplaces – some by top makers like Solon, others by replicas.

#12: 295 Sequoia c. 1918, Italian Renaissance.

#13: 1166 Martin c. 1906 Wolfe and McKenzie, architects. Local lore has that this home was built for Lewis Hanchett's mother, although we have not been able to fully document this yet. The home was featured in the original Hanchett Park advertising booklet. It is unique in that it has the stone fireplace on the front of the home. We do know that the next resident, William F. James, became a Superior Court Judge during his tenure on Martin Ave.

#14: 1163 Martin The Col House is one of Frank Wolfe's crown jewels. This home, along with the five Bungalow Row homes, has been documented inside and out by the Historic American Building Survey in 1978. It features matching leaded glass in the interior built ins, and is among the finest prairie design. It dates to 1913 and was built for Peter & Blanche Col. Peter Col was the Vice President of the Walsh-Col Company.

#15: 158 Tillman (at Sierra), a home that is the final rendition of one featured in the Hanchett Park advertising booklet. It was built in 1906 for the McGeogehan family and was designed by Wolfe and McKenzie. Wolfe's early work is classic craftsman (note the clinker brick accents, wood shingle siding, etc.)

#16: 1241 Sierra What we believe was Charlie Bigley's early home in the neighborhood. It's classic in its Craftsman style and unique with it's double porches, was merely a stepping stone to his palace on The Alameda where he hosted huge political barbecues and furthered his influence until his death in 1946. He resided here from 1926 until 1930. Charlie Bigley started out as a poor young man at the turn of the century, delivering a bakery route and dispensing favors. He got to know the working poor and he knew how to hustle. He opened a cigar store near the SP Depot on Bassett, and then started a taxi company that

A RESIDENCE STREET, SAN JOSE, CALIFORNIA.

Edith Corinne Smith Collection

evolved into an ambulance firm. When he lived here, he had opened his Bigley's Garage on South Market Street, right near the old City Hall.

Charlie Bigley was the man to see in San Jose if you needed a favor, or during the Depression if you needed a job. Historian Harry Farrell says Bigley took over City Hall by the rule of "select and elect". He bestowed favors on many and became a father figure to thousands who dutifully voted his slate. For years, he controlled four of the seven seats on the council, and the Bigley men met at the garage before each Council meeting to settle their business. His patronage was legendary. Long time SJ Police Chief Ray Blackmore was hired in 1929 because Bigley thought he was a hot prospect for the department ball team.

#17: **1299 Yosemite** A classic Prairie style, in the style immortalized by Frank Lloyd Wright, but prolifically used in San Jose by Frank D. Wolfe. We believe this home was built in 1914 for G.P. Nelson, a well driller.

#18: **1315, 23, and 31 Yosemite** Classic Hanchett Park Craftsman bungalows. The home at 1323 was featured in a movie around 1993 that starred Kirk Douglas and Craig T. Nelson.

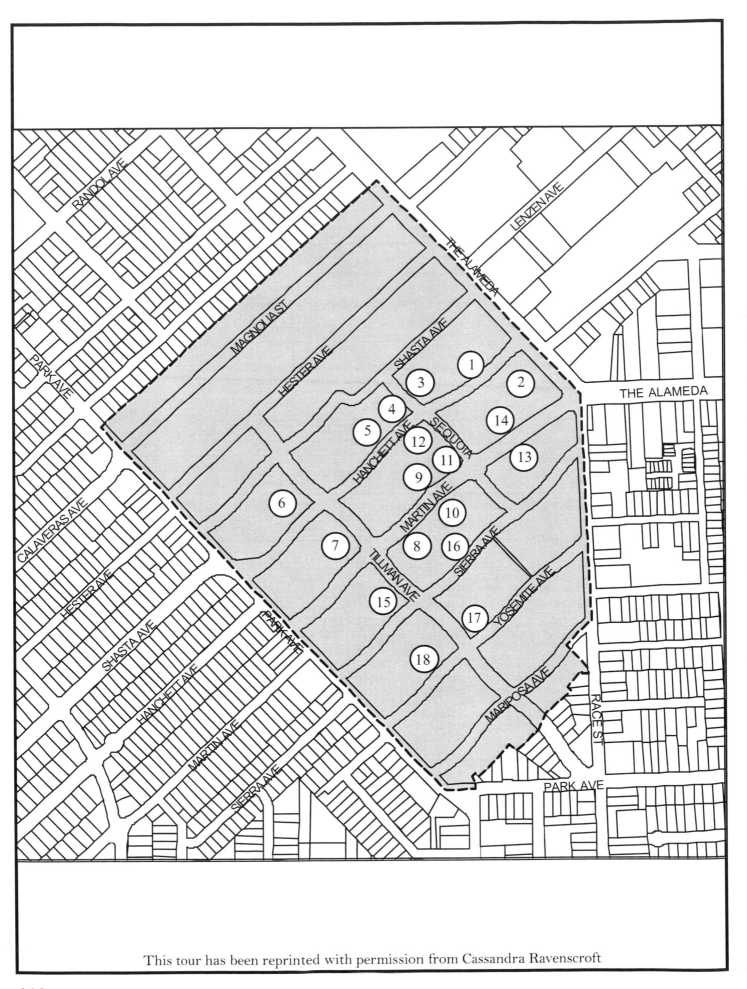

This tour has been reprinted with permission from Cassandra Ravenscroft

110

The Famous Alameda Blvd., SAN JOSE, Cal.

Tucker-Photo.

William A. Wulf

SCHURRA'S

840 The Alameda
San Jose, CA 95126
(408) 287-1562

"Creating a Tradition of Fine Chocolates Since 1912"

The Alameda's most historic candy store has been in existence since 1912. The Schurra family emigrated from France in 1881. Alphonse and Anna Mary Schurra traveled to America with their three-year-old daughter Mary, and one-year-old son Justin. On March 26, 1890, Anna Mary gave birth to a second son, Albert in the state of Washington. By 1910, Alphonse and Anna Mary were farming in Sunnyvale and Justin, age 30, was working as a steam engineer in San Francisco. Around this time, Albert married his first wife, Cecil, and Margaret was born the following year. In 1912, Albert reportedly opened his first of many candy shops in Stockton, California. In the following years, the Schurra brothers opened up to four more stores, serving buttercreams and peppermint chews all over Northern California. The details of Albert and Justin's very early candy-making enterprises are vague, but Justin Schurra opened The Alameda Confectionary on the Alameda in 1925 north of Hester Street, where the Shell Gas Station is right now. In 1933 Justin moved his candy store to Sunnyvale, near the old theater at 247 Murphy Avenue. In 1938, Justin and his wife Bessie closed the candy store to open a restaurant in a nearby location. It is said that Schurra brought the candy cases from the Sunnyvale shop to his new location at 848 The Alameda, which he opened in 1936. Albert sold the store to John A. Smith, who also had an ice cream shop at 205 South 2nd Street in San Jose. John Smith ran Schurra's Candy Factory at 848 The Alameda from 1942 through 1946, at which time he sold the business to Henry and Gayle Viehweger.

The next owner, Hank Viehweger, returned from war in 1945 with dreams of running a candy shop. The young man apprenticed Al Schurra for a year and bought the shop in 1946 using loans from his and his wife Gayle's parents.

During the war, Gayle would wait in line with her ration book at Schurra's so she could buy chocolates to send him in the South Pacific. While waiting for his candy fix to arrive, Hank would sneak into the ship's galley and create a peanut brittle concoction with a combination of sugar, corn syrup, and butter and any kind of nuts available. Hank put in 16-hour days until he approached retirement and sold the shop.

Schurra's occupied the 125-year old brick building on the corner of The Alameda and Sunol for four decades. Now, Brian Mundy continues almost a century of candy-making tradition in the European-style retail shop next-door. As in the last century, you can still watch the store-owner hand-decorate small batches of candy made with original recipes of the Schurra brothers. Just like The Alameda, Schurra's continues to improve and expand. It has a website and a new factory floor, but also honors its tradition of serving San Jose with high quality, hand-made candies.

Matteoni, O'Laughlin & Hechtman, Lawyers
848 The Alameda
San Jose, California 95126
Phone: (408) 293-4300
Fax: (408) 293-4004

This charming two-story brick commercial building was constructed between 1878 and 1881, with a first floor for commercial use and the upstairs for a residence. The earliest documented occupants were Charles and Frank Cleaves in 1881. In 1884, Joseph and Mrs. Mamie Cleaves were next to live there. Joseph was a clerk at a local hardware store, and Mamie was a teacher at Hester School. The Cleaves family owned much of the surrounding property on The Alameda, and now a street is named for them. In 1896, Edward and Jeremiah Cleaves resided in the second story of the building. Jeremiah used the office below for his well-boring company and Edward was a marble cutter. By the 1920's, the property was owned by Lewis Bohnett, a local attorney and State Assemblyman. VanDalsem Brothers Plumbing occupied the building in the 1930's.

In 1938, the building was sold to Albert Schurra. It was operated by him and subsequent parties as a candy store until 1999, when Bill and Marifran Mundy relocated it to an adjacent building. The building was designated a city landmark in 1992.

Photo by Rex Kuehner

In 2003, the building was remodeled as a law office by Norm Matteoni, Peggy O'Laughlin, Bradley Matteoni and Brian Matteoni (the first and second floors were integrated and an addition was placed at the back). The remodel was designed by James Ikeda, architect, and supervised by McLarney Construction, Inc., general contractor.

The structure is an Italianate style, red brick building with wide overhanging eaves and segmentally arched windows with bracketed and pedimented hoods. The transomed storefront display windows are framed by cast iron pilasters, imprinted with "F. Altman," made by the Altman Foundry of San Jose, which was established in 1878. The building is an example of rare 19th century commercial architecture in San Jose. The law firm of Matteoni, O'Laughlin & Hechtman, which specializes in condemnation and land use, currently occupies the building

Greenlee's Bakery
1081 The Alameda
San Jose, CA 95126
(408) 287-4191

Since 1924

A passing century has left behind memory of the mansions that stood at the bend near Race Street. As early as 1876, the Tisdale mansion occupied the land where Greenlee's now stands. In Vignettes of the Gardens of San Jose de Guadalupe, Edward R. Polhemus describes,

> Facing Agriculture Park was another district of impressive homes. The William Tisdale family lived at the turn of the road. From the pointed iron fence, lawns and pathways led to the house. Scattered specimen shrubs and trees grew there, among them, oleanders, lemon verbena, and snowball have been recalled. Next door came the Alexander Yoell home, featuring palm trees; while adjoining, was the Woodson property with its beautiful magnolias.

Frank Mitchell Greenlee and Harriett J. Greenlee moved to San Jose in 1925 with their son Emmett Greenlee. Frank and Harriett were Kansas natives and had two more children after coming to

Sue (Williams) Bebb and her husband, Robert S. Bebb at their wedding reception at Hotel St. Clair on August 7, 1948, cutting into a Greenlee's cake together

San Jose—Myron and Helen. Frank M. Greenlee himself constructed this building in the 1920's. Emmett operated the bakery until he sold it to Rosalinda and Norbert Geldner in 1981. The Geldner family continues the age-old family tradition of baking handcrafted pastries. Almost eighty years later, Greenlee's bakery continues to entice the occasional passerby with its aromatic sticky-cinnamon loafs.

The baking staff begins as early as 2 or 3 a.m. with the Danishes, turnovers, coffeecakes and burnt almond cakes. Greenlee's has culturally expanded from its Midwestern origins. Rosalinda came to the United States from Mexico when she was twelve, and Norbert emigrated from Germany. Customers can start their day with either a chorizo breakfast burrito, or cinnamon bread made from Norbert's German recipe. As one of the two oldest businesses on The Alameda, the bakery's cheerful atmosphere will surely be serving these returning faces for years to come.

Café Rosalena
1077 The Alameda
San Jose, CA 95126
(408) 287-2400

To the left: Larry Leighton waters his front lawn in back of the Fredkin's parking lot.

To the right: a cart full of flowers sits in front of Bettencourt's the successor to Fredkin's.

Café Rosalena is a well-known breakfast and lunch destination for locals. This was a favorite lunch spot in the '30's, as well. At this same location, the Hester Pharmacy was a popular lunch place among children from Hester School. One graduate from Hester School fondly recalls, "They had a special table at the drugstore at noon for kids. My folks would give me 21 cents—a dime for a sandwich and a dime for a milkshake, a big one, and a penny for sales tax." The Hester Pharmacy, a grocery store and meat market, was constructed in the late 1920's. The Alameda Pharmacy took its place in the late 1930's.

Adjacent to the building that Café Rosalena now occupies was a 15-room mansion built in 1860. The mansion was set back from the street with an impressive front yard. The Waddington family purchased it in 1920 from Charles Parkinson. Mrs. Waddington took great pains to plant ivy, shrubs, and other trees to conceal stucco walls of grocery stores on either side of her 100-foot garden. The grocery store in-between Rosalena's and the Waddington Property was Fredkin's Grocery Store. Fredkin's opened in the 1940's. It was known for selling peanut butter in bulk out of a big barrel. It later became Bettencourt's Market. The grocery store on the other side of the Waddington property was Safeway, originally the Piggly Wiggly Market.

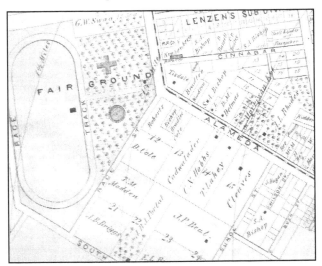

Thompson & West Historical Atlas

The bend at Race Street in 1878.

According to Mrs. George M. Smith, the daughter of Mrs. Waddington, there were magnolia trees on the property that had a spread of close to 50 feet. The Woodsons later owned this mansion, which had 15 rooms and two magnolia trees at the entrance. These magnolia trees became the two biggest magnolia trees in the state of California by 1946.

Westminster Presbyterian Church
1100 Shasta Ave, San Jose CA, 95126
(408) 294-7447
www.westpres-sj.org

Westminster Presbyterian Church traces roots to the first Protestant church in San Jose. Reverend John Douglas organized the Independent Presbyterian Church with a band of six Christian pioneer families on October 7, 1849. It adopted a more fitting name in 1858—the First Presbyterian Church of San Jose. Its first permanent church structure was built in 1851 on North Second Street. When the congregation outgrew the church, with 669 attendees by 1890, a second church was built. A branch congregation of 105 parishioners dedicated the Second Presbyterian Church on September 13, 1891.

After almost thirty years, the spirit of the congregation began to surpass the quality of its house of worship. On September 27, 1920, the Board of Trustees declared that the dilapidated old church was in such a state of disrepair that it was detrimental to the growth of church membership.

A committee was elected to locate a site to meet the most needs of our community, particularly in the newly developed Hanchett Hester area, across from Fredericksburg Brewery and just north of the fair grounds and race track. The building, designed in the arts and crafts mission style by architect, Carl Werner, was completed in 1927 at a cost of $54,327.

The church members voted to change its name to Westminster to reflect its new location as the church on the west side of town. The stained class windows which were brought over from the old Second Church are judged to be the finest in San Jose. The two manual keyboard pipe organ was built in the early 1920s to accompany silent films in the Roosevelt Theater of Los Angeles. It has over a thousand pipes and nineteen different instrument voices.

Westminster Church was established as a Christian presence in its neighborhood and it continues to invite the community to worship and serve God. It offers its facilities to neighborhood groups and to The Alameda business community. It hosts the annual Christmas Tree lighting and plays a major role in the Farmers Market that meets at the Downtown College Prep.

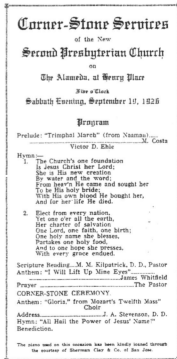

Corner-Stone Services
of the New
Second Presbyterian Church
on
The Alameda, at Henry Place
Five o'Clock
Sabbath Evening, September 19, 1926

Program

Prelude: "Trimphal March" (from Naaman)......................M. Costa
Victor D. Ehle
Hymn:—
1.   The Church's one foundation
     Is Jesus Christ her Lord;
     She is His new creation
     By water and the word;
     From heav'n He came and sought her
     To be His holy bride;
     With His own blood He bought her,
     And for her life He died.

2.   Elect from every nation,
     Yet one o'er all the earth,
     Her charter of salvation
     One Lord, one faith, one birth;
     One holy name she blesses,
     Partakes one holy food,
     And to one hope she presses,
     With every grace endued.

Scripture Reading....M. M. Kilpatrick, D. D., Pastor
Anthem: "I Will Lift Up Mine Eyes"..................
.....................................James Whitfield
Prayer ....The Pastor
CORNER-STONE CEREMONY.
Anthem: "Gloria," from Mozart's Twelfth Mass"
Choir
Address................................J. A. Stevenson, D. D.
Hymn: "All Hail the Power of Jesus' Name!"
Benediction.

The piano used on this occasion has been kindly loaned through
the courtesy of Sherman Clay & Co. of San Jose.

 **YMCA** *of* **Santa Clara Valley** We build **STRONG** kids, STRONG *families* & STRONG *communities.*

Central YMCA
1717 The Alameda, San Jose, CA 95126
(408) 298-1717
www.scvymca.org/central

First coming to San Jose in 1867, the YMCA echoed Father Catala's motives of developing the Christian character of San Jose. There were still lots of saloons in San Jose when the YMCA first rented rooms in the Messing Building on South First Street. At first, the YMCA facilities were comprised of a conference room and a reading room. Now, the YMCA of San Jose has grown to seven branches and has more than 30,000 members and 3,000 volunteers in the Santa Clara Valley. Annually, more than 8,000 people participate in camp, sports, swim lessons, teen programs and other activities at the Central YMCA. As the largest not-for-profit community-based organization in America, YMCA leaders invented basketball, volleyball and racquetball, and pioneered camping, physical fitness and swimming lessons.

In 1867, the YMCA immediately embarked upon its first project—to open San Jose's first public library. By July, the library was scheduling lectures and had collected over 800 volumes. In 1872, the City of San Jose assumed the YMCA's debts (about $600) in exchange for the library books and its furnishings.

The YMCA changed locations multiple times towards the end of the century. By 1886, the YMCA's facilities included a gym, a vaulting horse, rings, chest weights, and a boxing mat. Classes in bookkeeping, French and German, penmanship, and vocal music were offered. In the 1890s, there was a YMCA bicycle club. In 1913, the YMCA moved to a new building on the corner of Third and Santa Clara. The YMCA also fed the hungry and had rooms upstairs where young men could live temporarily. Service men were offered free memberships during the world war times. This facility is still standing as a San Jose landmark.

In 1938, the YMCA ran into financial trouble, with increasing debts and low membership income. Secretary Dahlquist reported to the Board of Directors that the Y's greatest problem was that it had not expanded its facilities since its opening. As a result, the board consummated the purchase of 60 acres for a campsite near Boulder Creek. In 1940, they renovated the building built in 1913.

In 1953 the YMCA purchased the Borchers, Webb, Hart, Coolidge, and de Bourguinon properties. Among others, John D. Crummey and Alex L. Hart led a 1955 campaign for funds to build the current facility on these 3.5 acres. A sundial that was originally part of the landscaping of the Hart mansion can still be seen in the courtyard behind the YMCA building. Since then, the YMCA has continued to flourish and strengthen the community around The Alameda.

Bellarmine College Preparatory
960 W. Hedding St.
San Jose, CA. 95126
(408) 294-9224
www.bcp.org

Bellarmine College Preparatory, a Jesuit secondary school, was founded by Father John Nobili, S.J., in 1851 as Santa Clara College, a school for secondary and college age students. In the early 1920's, Santa Clara College was renamed to separate the two schools and became Santa Clara University and Santa Clara Prep. In 1925, Santa Clara Prep moved from the grounds of the University to our current location at Hedding and Elm. In 1926, Santa Clara Prep changed its name to Bellarmine College Preparatory in honor of Robert Cardinal Bellarmine, a Jesuit of the sixteenth century who recently had been canonized a saint and recongnized as a Doctor of the Church. In 2001, Bellarmine celebrated its 150th anniversary as a Jesuit secondary school.

Law Offices of Linda Silveria
Certified Specialist in Probate, Estate Planning and Trust Law
2021 The Alameda # 110
San Jose, CA 95126-1126
(408) 985-2500

Sourisseau Academy

The bicycling craze hit its peak during the 1890s, but cyclers had begun competing on the Race Track in the Agricultural Park the decade before. On April 19, 1895, the County of Santa Clara opened its first cement velodrome at the intersection of what is now Race Street and Park Avenue. As a main attraction at the Agricultural Park, the velodrome had an ellipse-shaped track that was one third mile long. Its curves were sloped at 20-degrees. It cost $9,000 to build and became "became the site of many world-class races." Lewis E. Hanchett purchased the Agricultural Park for a residential subdivision in 1906.

San Jose's sixth velodrome, the Burbank velodrome, was built in 1936 a couple blocks away from the first velodrome. Also known as the Garden City Velodrome, the Burbank Velodrome was uncovered in 2004 when Lincoln High School remodeled its football field.

Attorney Linda Silveria, currently practicing on The Alameda, is a descendant of multiple San Jose bicyclists, including Mel Silvera, Cecilia Silvera, and Isabel Silvera. Cecilia and Isabel, Linda's aunts, were notable female racers at the Burbank Velodrome in 1936. Mel Silvera began racing at the Burbank Velodrome at the age of 17. He not only achieved fame as an amateur who turned professional at a young age, but he was also famous for being a one-armed bicyclist!

Mel Silvera devised special handlebars to accommodate his stump-arm. This special equipment placed him on equal footing with other cyclists in most races, but could not compensate for a disadvantage in team races. Frequently, the Burbank Velodrome held six-day races, marathon versions of the team races. Silvera's disability did not seem to affect his amateur career, but probably caused his rapid disappearance from the professional ranks.

In January 1937, Mel Silvera attended a six-day race in San Francisco. He was unable to finish the race due to painful saddle sores caused by resting his weight entirely on one hand during sprints.

Perseverance is a Silvera family trait. Linda Silvera provides her clients the best legal advice and representation with the same determination as her bicycle-racing ancestors.

HABANA CUBA
r e s t a u r a n t

238 Race Street, San Jose CA, 95126
408-998-CUBA (2822)
www.998cuba.com

Race Street has been home to Habana Cuba Restaurant since 1994 and is now one of the "Top 50 Hispanic Restaurants in the Country"(Hispanic Magazine). Enchanting neighbors and visitors with its homey, slow roasting cooking, Habana Cuba has become a local favorite. Who knew that they would eventually become one of the most "Romantic" Restaurants in the Bay Area (SJ Mercury News 2006)!

Appropriately, this property was once owned by the romantic bon vivant Henry Morris Naglee. In the 1870s, Naglee owned 140 acres adjacent to The Alameda. In 1859, he sold 76 of these acres to the Agricultural Society for use as the Agricultural Park. Race Street, where Habana Cuba is located, is named for the racetrack that was once part of this park.

General Henry Morris Naglee was one of the most distinguished citizens in San Jose. He was a graduate of West Point and served in the Mexican War as well as the Civil War. After helping to found the first banking house in San Francisco, Naglee moved to San Jose in 1858. He became a pioneer viticulturist in San Jose and produced his own Brandy. Naglee was also central in the establishment of Alum Rock Park.

Soon after Naglee arrived in San Jose, he met a woman named Mary Schell at a party. An intriguing love affair ensued. Though Naglee left San Jose for a few years, the couple maintained a passionate and vigorous love correspondence. Each letter began with "Chere Petite" or "Dear dear baby" or "My own dear, darling little one." In one letter, he wrote, "Dear Baby, are we not well mated? Was ever man and woman more completely so? Have we not loved, and loved and grown lean and fattened on love? Have we not whispered love with all its sweetest accents, unintelligible but to the very, very few that have loved as we have loved?"

Naglee went to Europe in 1860 to study viticulture and to bring back vines and briefly visited San Jose again before leaving to join the Union Forces on the East Coast. He became a hero at the Battle of Fair Oaks in May of 1862. He returned to San Francisco in 1865 and sent Mary Schell a final letter, which began with "My Dear Friend." Mary read on to discover a greatly disappointing message. "I have been quite unwell since my arrival, but not ill enough to be confined to my room. I have not called again, for the reason that I have no intention to interrupt any of your friendly associations so agreeably established. I shall always be most happy to know that you are doing well."

Due to this sudden and unexpected dismissal, Mary Schell took revenge on the General. In 1867, she published The Love Life of Brigadier General Henry M. Naglee, Consisting of a Correspondence on Love, War, and Politics. The book included all of the letters that she had received from him through the years.

James B. Randol owned 218 acres surrounding Randol Avenue, called the Randol Addition. During his years in Santa Clara County, Randol acquired some 600 acres of land. He invested wisely in business transactions and was a leading stockholder of the prominent Vendrome Hotel in San Jose. It was said that Randol "was an imaginative and creative individual that functioned in business transactions with logic and practical solutions." What used to be the Randol Addition is now occupied in part by Dave Samuels with Sentra Securities. One might think to apply such a statement to both Samuels and Randol—one an investor on The Alameda today, and one an investor of the past.

As an independent Certified Financial Planner™ professional and Accredited Investment Fiduciary, Dave is thoroughly familiar with wealth transfer from generation to generation, and estate planning issues. Years of experience and investment knowledge enable Dave Samuels to create the best strategy in ensuring a lasting legacy for your family.

In July 1870, J. B. Randol arrived in New Almaden as the newly appointed general manager of the Quicksilver Mines. In New York, he had been secretary of the Quicksilver Mining Company for seven years. He was thirty-four with no previous management experience or any technical knowledge of mining operations. The future success of the mines depended on Randol. Prior to his arrival, inefficiencies in production and decrease of income had led to debt. Randol immediately sprung to action in saving the mines. He solicited financial subscriptions and gathered $200,000 for a working fund. He hired engineers to design more efficient furnaces and initiated construction of a new shaft to expand quicksilver exploration. He is most widely known for raising standards of working conditions there and reshaping life in the mining community. He strove to create the ideal community for the employees at the mines. By establishing the strictest routine of economical production, he set the mines on the track to success and also emphasized having the most efficient workers for specific types of work. Randol resigned in March 1892 and died in 1903 after returning to New York.

1146 Randol Street
San Jose CA, 95126

Once part of J. B. Randol's Addition to the Chapman and Davis Tract, the Clara Louise Lawrence Residence at 1146 Randol Street remains a historic craftsman bungalow near The Alameda. Harold C. Hayes, an automobile salesman, constructed this house in about 1921. After living there for a year, he then moved to Martin Avenue and sold the home to Clara Louise Lawrence. According to Charlene Duval, Clara Louise Lawrence, an Ohio native, was a popular poet and writer of children's stories. Her first work, a collection of poems, was published in Pennsylvania in 1914. She moved to Santa Clara with her husband John Jacob Lawrence Sr. in 1922. While living at 1146 Randol Street between 1922 and 1942, Clara wrote The Sea Witch and Other Stories and Poems for Children. Starting in 1923, Clara ran her own "circulating library" in the Ryland block of downtown San Jose. A year later, Clara, Miriam, Kathryn and Mrs. B K Beverson operated a "Wisteria Tea House" at 1043 The Alameda. As a valuable member of San Jose Poetry Club, Clara published Poems Along the Way, in 1927. This work included her famous poem, "Valley of Heart's Delight"

The Santa Clara Valley is
To those who hold it dear
A veritable Paradise
Each season of the year.
One loves it best in April
When the fruit-trees are in bloom;
And a mass of snowy blossoms
Yield a subtle sweet perfume.
When orchard after orchard
Is spread before the eyes
With the whitest of white blossoms
Neath the bluest of blue skies.
No brush could paint the picture
No pen describe the sight
That one can find in April
In "The Valley of Heart's Delight."

"Poems Along the Way" by Clara Louise Lawrence [copyright 1927, published by Tucker Printing Company, San Jose, California]

In 1942 Clara sold the home to A. W. Margraf and his wife Lucille. Clara passed away in 1950.

Dunham & Associates, CPAs
1884 The Alameda
San Jose, CA 95126
(408) 260-9600
www.dunhamcpas.com

Quality. Service. Ethics.

Dunham & Associates, CPAs are committed to offering a level of service that exceeds expectations. They provide quality work in a timely manner for tax and accounting needs. Dunham & Associates, CPAs is located in the old Mediterranean-style mansion on 1884 The Alameda. Jessie H. Turner deeded this land to Ida A. Jordan in 1916, when the house was probably built. The renowned Allen T. Gilliland bought the house around 1944.

Allen Gilliland was a modern-day pioneer on The Alameda. He was an entrepreneur with a vision that he boldly turned into reality. He started out in the bakery business with his father, but in 1955 received a license for San Jose's first television station—Channel 11. When Gill Industries formed a partnership with San Jose Cable TV, the energetic 41-year-old sold the Sunlite Bakery to focus on his vision of an integrated communications system.

In 1966, cable television was an innovative field much like the Internet was in the '90s. One *Mercury News* writer marveled at Gilliland's idea that by 1976 "your 20 TV channels would carry everything from adult education to high-school football to regular television programming." A. T. Gilliland strived make this dream come true for San Jose and began construction of the cable system in 1970.

Gill Cable is credited as "one of the forerunners of top quality cable TV." In 1982 it brought 58 channels to San Jose and Campbell, a number that towered over Viacom's measly 30 channels in San Francisco. Gill Cable was the first cable system to offer movies without commercials as part of its basic cable service. The first movie Gill Cable showed was *Towering Inferno*. Like Dunham & Associates CPAs, Gilliland did not hesitate to serve his clients services with the highest possible quality.

In 1976 the system passed 155,000 dwelling units, with a 36% penetration. Gill Cable had 64,000 customers. By the '80s, Gill Cable alone was the largest, independent, locally owned cable system in the country.

In 1982, Gill Cable entered into a contract with Viacom from San Francisco, creating the nation's largest regional cable television network.

Gill was the first one to see the feasibility of the cable network and jumped at the opportunity he found. As a result, his successful company initiated cable in the San Jose area and made it possible for people to see the world through so many channels in the '70s and '80s.

919 The Alameda
San Jose, CA 95126
(408) 350-7500
www.creditcorp.com

Technology Credit Corporation (TCC) now occupies what used to be the Rhodes residence. Judge Augustus L. Rhodes lived in a two-story house imported around the Cape Horn from the East Coast. When Hiram Shartzer set up The Alameda Turnpike Company, Judge A. L Rhodes was one of the first five residents on The Alameda. As a prominent San Jose attorney and judge, Rhodes signed multiple petitions pertaining to The Alameda. One petition that he signed called for preserving the center row of trees when Bishop built his electric streetcar. This petition failed, and the trees were removed "secretly at night" to make way for the streetcar. However, Rhodes' objection to building the streetcar there is peculiar because he assisted Bishop in building a railroad on First Street.

Fisher Insulators owned by Colin Jung

TCC finances high-tech equipment sold by vendor clients, making it easy for clients to sell to their customers. In 1888, TCC would have been the company to finance technology like the Fisher insulator that Bishop and Rich used in their underground streetcar. Bishop financed innovation when he brought the Frank E. Fisher to San Jose to create the Fisher insulator.

When Bishop and Rich set out to find a model for their electric railroad, they did not know exactly what they were looking for. They traveled to Denver, Kansas City, Windsor, Canada, Baltimore and Detroit, searching far and wide for any streetcar system that could satisfy government officials. In Detroit, they found Frank E. Fisher at work on a streetcar system in Highland Park. They hired Fisher to modify his system and satisfy the safety concerns of the Town of Santa Clara. The Fisher System used a third, center rail for its electric power, and Fisher re-designed it to be buried below the ground, which they expected to be safer. To improve the current-carrying capacity in the center rail, Fisher designed the underground rail with a copper wire that improved its current-carrying capacity. Glass insulators held the third rail and mounted the power line. The insulators that Fisher designed for The Alameda were short-lived, yet extremely valuable as part of the second electric streetcar in California.

In the 1960s, ceramic materials began to replace glass because they were lightweight and less costly. Now glass insulators are popular collector's items—especially the Fisher Insulators. Fisher Insulators were unique in color and design, and were only used by Detroit Electrical Works and in Bishop's line. The *Guide to North American Glass Pintype Insulators* quotes that a single aqua or ice blue Fisher insulator is worth $4,500 to $5,000, and a single lime green Fisher insulator is worth $5,000 to $7,500!

1342 Naglee Avenue
San Jose, CA 95191
Phone: (408) 947-3600
Fax: (408) 947-3677
www.egyptianmuseum.org

The Rosicrucian Egyptian Museum houses the largest collection of genuine ancient Egyptian artifacts on display in western North America, and is the only such museum built in the Egyptian style. The Museum strives to convey everything that can be reliably known about its artifacts and the roles that the artifacts played in Egyptian history. AMORC encourages visitors to consider how a historical artifact, event, or person reveals some truth about humanity and the nature of the world.

The Case of the Mummy Who Knew the Way to San Jose...

A Rosicrucian member in Texas was reading the Neiman-Marcus Christmas catalog in 1971 and noticed a pair of "His and Her" mummy cases for sale. The Rosicrucian Egyptian Museum promptly rescued these artifacts so they might be properly conserved and displayed as revered human funerary relics. When the mummy cases arrived from England, the US customs x-ray process in Florida revealed that one case was occupied! Police investigations confirmed that this body was not the result of a crime, and the antiquity of the ancient stowaway was established. In 1995, examinations of the mummy revealed an iron pin in the mummy's leg. In 2002, the National Geographic Channel's "Mummy Road Show" filmed an episode at the Museum, doing extensive non-invasive forensic testing, which indicated that the mummy might be from either the Roman period, or from the 19th-20th Dynasties (ca. 1200 – 1000 BCE).

CLEOPATRA'S NEEDLE AND PLANETARIUM IN ROSICRUCIAN PARK, SAN JOSE, CALIFORNIA   462

History San José

This rose-red obelisk, capped with copper, is a three-quarter size replica of the original, which stood before the House of the Sun in Heliopolis – the Biblical city of "On," also known as "Annu" in 2300 BCE. The hieroglyphs say in part "Horus, the one born of life. King of the North and the South, Kheper-Ka-Ra."

The most recent research has been done on the Museum's Child Mummy using hi-tech scanning at Stanford Medical Center under a joint project with Stanford University, Silicon Graphics, and the NASA Biocomputational Lab in 2005. Over 60,000 scans revealed much about the physiology of the little girl who was lovingly buried by her grieving parents approximately 2,000 years ago. The project shows the cutting edge of technology for delving into the mysteries of our past, while respecting the integrity of this very human legacy. These mummies can still be visited **for free** in the Rosicrucian Museum!

Avalon ON THE Alameda

Time Well Spent®

Pollard Willows near University Avenue

History San José

Rose Garden Resident
1095 The Alameda
San Jose, CA. 95126
(408) 200-1030 (direct)
(408) 200-1012 (fax)

Silicon Valley Community Newspapers, which is located on The Alameda in the heart of the Rose Garden neighborhood, publishes nine weekly community newspapers in Santa Clara County. At one time, the company was a part of Metro Newspapers, but became a completely independent company in December 2001 when David Cohen, who co-founded Metro in 1985, bought out his business partners and became publisher/CEO of the Community Newspapers. In the summer of 2006, Silicon Valley Community Newspapers became a part of Media News.

The nine weekly newspapers reach more than 170,000 homes in specific geographic areas of the valley with news specific to that area. Coverage includes local schools, youth sports, business, law enforcement, features and community profiles as well as the impact of local government on the community. In each of the weekly newspapers, the opinion pages serve as a forum for community dialogue about local issues.

Each of the newspapers is committed to coverage that is "fiercely local" within each circulation area. The nine community newspapers are: the Los Gatos Weekly-Times, Saratoga News, Cupertino Courier, Sunnyvale Sun, Campbell Reporter, Willow Glen Resident, Almaden Resident, West San Jose Resident, and, of course, the coverage wouldn't be complete without a newspaper for the residents of the Rose Garden.

Here is a brief history of that newspaper, the Rose Garden Resident:

On May 8, 2003, Community Newspapers launched its second "Resident," this time serving the greater Rose Garden area of San Jose, an area bordered roughly by Highway 880 and W. San Carlos Street and Stockton and Winchester. The first "Resident" was the Willow Glen Resident. The Rose Garden debuted to an enthusiastic readership. From the start, readers made it clear that they were excited to finally have their own community newspaper.

Residents of the greater Rose Garden area are proud of their heritage and their diversity, and they were eager to share their stories with the newspaper. By August of that year, Community Newspapers was able to add a sports section to its coverage of school, community and neighborhood news.

Visit us online at: www.community-newspapers.com

--Community Newspapers

J. LOHR

VINEYARDS & WINES

1000 Lenzen Avenue
San Jose, CA 95126
(408) 288-5057
www.jlohr.com

Viticulture on The Alameda traces its beginnings to California Governor De Neve who promoted the planting of grapevines and fruit trees in the early days of the Santa Clara Mission. Farming was an immediate success in the fertile Santa Clara Valley but it was obvious that tending vineyards required special care and expertise. Explorer Vancouver witnessed orchards, vineyards, and fields at the mission but sadly noted the "failure of the vine" during his visit to the area in 1792. Subsequently, the mission enjoyed success and produced the first wine in the Santa Clara Valley in 1802. Since then, mission vines became "historic for their strong growth and abundant fruitage." When Duflot de Mofras visited Santa Clara in 1840, he observed that the vineyards were "proving successful, although their cultiation [sic] has been neglected by the colonists." By 1827, the county was producing 800 gallons of wine per year, and 3,721 gallons wine by 1860.

Jeff Meier and Jerry Lohr

The Pacific Wine Company, located on The Alameda a century ago, established a tradition of winemaking on The Alameda. In 1890, the Pacific Wine Company produced 400,000 gallons of wine here on The Alameda. Less than a century later in the early 70s, Jerry Lohr of J. Lohr Vineyards & Wines located his winery adjacent to The Alameda at the site of the former Falstaff Brewery. He brought his knowledge--gained from his extensive farming background--of soil conditions and climates optimal for winegrowing and winemaking. From 3,000 acres of estate grapes grown in Paso Robles, Monterey County and Napa Valley, J. Lohr now produces a comprehensive portfolio of world-class wines, including J. Lohr Estates, J. Lohr Vineyard Series, J. Lohr Cuvée Series and Cypress Vineyards, among others. Interestingly, J. Lohr even produces a non-alcoholic wine, ARIEL, which has won gold medals competing with wines containing alcohol. The J. Lohr San Jose Wine Center is open to the public every day from 10-5 and can provide an intimate venue for private parties and events.

Plant 51
88 Bush Street
Sales Office at 734 The Alameda

Not Just Living History.   History You Can Live In.

Fifty One. Distinctive one and two bedroom Condos, Lofts and Townhomes by Centex Homes. Located in the heart of downtown San Jose just off the Alameda at 88 Bush Street, Fifty One doesn't have to fake the hip industrial look.

It started life in 1913 as a dried fruit packing factory, contributing a significant chapter to San Jose's history as an agricultural capital. In 1917, the building's owner, Calpak (California Packing Corporation) chose the brand name Del Monte to market its products across the country. Del Monte thus became the first national canned food brand.

Nearly a hundred years later, it's becoming San Jose's hottest new center of urban living. This careful restoration includes building a completely new foundation to support the original brick structure. The finished homes at Fifty One will combine sleek architecture with the original warehouse walls. Retro chic meets modern style at Fifty One.

You'll find Fifty One just off The Alameda, near the HP Pavilion, downtown restaurants, urban shopping and transportation including CalTrain, VTA light rail, HWY 280 and HWY 880.

Original brick walls in some of the new condo/lofts are reminiscent of Fifty One's historic past as Del Monte Plant 51. Clean lines and modern comforts offer a sophisticated and eclectic lifestyle.

Fifty One—offering new homes in downtown San Jose. (Even though it's almost a hundred years old.)

CENTEX HOMES
Built to a Higher Standard

133

Notes

Introduction

1. "Historic Santa Clara Road is Community Milennium Trail," City of Santa Clara, http://www.ci.santa-clara.ca.us/about_us/history05.html (accessed Sept. 3, 2006).

2. "Three Historic Alameda Willows Marked, Blessed," *The Mercury Herald*, May 5, 1934. Santa Clara University Archives: Spearman Papers.

3. "In 'The Good Old Days'—Here and Elsewhere," *San Jose Mercury News*, Nov 18, 1934.

Origins of The Alameda

1. Lawrence H. Shoup and Randall Milliken, *Inigo of Rancho Posolmi: The Life and Times of A Mission Indian and His Land* (Menlo Park: Ballena Press, 1999), 46.

2. Fr. Francisco M. Sanches and Fr. Magin Catalá, "Informe," (December 31, 1795). Available from: Arthur Spearman, *The Five Franciscan Churches of Mission Santa Clara* (Palo Alto: National Press, 1963), 48.

3. Arthur. D. Spearman, S.J. December 14, 1969. Santa Clara University Archives: Spearman Papers, folder 39.

4. Clarence Urmy, "Old Willows of 'The Alameda,' Their Past and Present in Poetry and Prose," *The Mercury Herald*, Sept. 9, 1917.

5. "Three Historic Alameda Willows Marked, Blessed," *The Mercury Herald*, May 5, 1934. Santa Clara University Archives: Spearman Papers.

6. Eugene T. Sawyer, *History of Santa Clara County*, California (Los Angeles: Historic Record Company, 1922), 283.

7. Lorie Garcia, George Giacomini, and Geoffrey Goodfellow, *A Place of Promise* ed. Tony DiMarco (Santa Clara: City of Santa Clara, 2002), 48.

8. Gregory B. McCandless, "The Alameda of San Jose: A Historical Land Use and Development Study" (Masters thesis presented to the Department of Urban and Regional Planning, San Jose State University, 1988), 12.

9. Patricia Loomis, *Signposts* (San Jose, CA: San Jose Historical Museum Association, 1982), 11.

10. William F. James and George H. McMurry, *History of San Jose, California, Narrative and Biographical* (San Jose, CA: Smith Printing Company, 1933), 25.

11. James, 31.

12. Mark G. Hylkema, *Archeological Investigations at the Third Location of Mission Santa Clara de Asis* (Oakland: Caltrans District 4 Environmental Planning, 1995), 51.

13. Road Files, "Hester's Complaint against The Alameda Road" Letter by Judge Craven P Hester to the Board of Supervisors, March 9, 1864.

14. Oscar O. Winther, *The Story of San Jose, 1777-1869* (San Francisco: California Historical Society, 1935), 7.

15. Winther, 11.

16. Shoup, 50.

17. Stephen M. Payne, *Santa Clara County: Harvest of Change* (Northridge: Windsor Publications, 1987), 25.

18. James, 25

19. Winther, 9.

20. Ralph Rambo, *Almost Forgotten* (Santa Clara: 1964), 9.

Willows

1. City of San Jose's Department of City Planning, *The Alameda* (San Jose: 1984), 11.

2. Patricia Loomis, *Signposts* (San Jose, CA: San Jose Historical Museum Association, 1982), 12.

3. Chester S. Lyman, *Around the Horn to the Sandwich Islands and California, 1845-1850* ed. Frederick J. Teggart (New Haven: Yale University Press, 1924), 217, 230-231.

4. "City May Replant Trees On Alameda," *San Jose Mercury News*, April 12, 1938.

5. William K. Ingraham, *Early Days of My Episcopate* (Oakland: Biobooks, 1954), 62.

6 Helen W. Kennedy and Kinzie K. Veronica, *Vignettes of the Gardens of San Jose de Guadalupe* (San Jose: San Jose Garden Club, 1938), 19.

7 Arthur D. Spearman, S.J. December 14, 1969. Santa Clara University Archives: Spearman Papers, folder 39.

8 "Three Historic Alameda Willows Marked, Blessed," *The Mercury Herald*, May 5, 1934. Santa Clara University Archives: Spearman Papers.

9 Arthur D. Spearman, Caption for a photo of The Alameda, 1869. Santa Clara University Archives.

10 William F. James and George H. McMurry, *History of San Jose, California, Narrative and Biographical* (San Jose, CA: Smith Printing Company, 1933), 39.

11 Dorothy F. Regnery, *The Battle of Santa Clara* (San Jose: Smith and McKay Printing Company, 1978), 54.

12 Theron G. Cady, "Tales of the San Francisco Peninsula," *Peninsula Life Magazine*, 1948, http://www. sfgenealogy.com/sanmateo/history/smcady_c.htm (accessed Sept. 12, 2006).

Father Magin de Catalá

1 Zephyrin Engelhardt, *The Holy Man of Santa Clara: Life, Virtues and Miracles of Fr. Magín Catalá, O.F.M.* (San Francisco: J. H. Barry, 1909), 3.

2 "The Life of Father Magin Catalá," Santa Clara University Archives: Spearman Papers, folder 45.

3 Ralph Rambo, *Almost Forgotten* (Santa Clara: 1964), 32.

4 Engelhardt, 161

5 Engelhardt, 148.

6 Engelhardt, 150.

7 Clyde Arbuckle, *Clyde Arbuckle's History of San José* ed. Leonard McKay (San Jose: Smith and McKay Printing Company, 1986), 94.

Transportation

Edith B. Webb, *Indian Life at the Old Missions* (Los Angeles: W.F. Lewis, 1952), 270.

1 Oscar O. Winther, *The Story of San Jose, 1777-1869* (San Francisco: California Historical Society, 1935), 36.

2 Winther, 37.

3 Arbuckle, 114.

4 "Chain of Ownership," A.P.N 261-9-018. Notes by Scott Soper.

5 Charles S. McCaleb, *Tracks, Tires & Wires* (Glendale: Interurban Press, 1891), 14.

6 Helen W. Kennedy and Kinzie K. Veronica, *Vignettes of the Gardens of San Jose de Guadalupe* (San Jose: San Jose Garden Club, 1938), 7.

7 Charles S. McCaleb, *The San Jose Railroads: Centennial 1868-1968*, (Foothill Junior College District, 1968), 3.

8 Gregory B. McCandless, "The Alameda of San Jose: A Historical Land Use and Development Study" (Masters thesis presented to the Department of Urban and Regional Planning, San Jose State University, 1988), 13.

9 H. S. Foote, *Pen Pictures from the Garden of the World of Santa Clara County California* (Chicago, IL: The Lewis Publishing Company, 1888), 120.

10 "St. Joseph's Church Bulletin," n.d. Santa Clara University Archives: Spearman Papers.

11 Board of Directors to the Board of Supervisors, "In the matter of the Alameda Turnpike Road Company: Proposal to Sell to the County," May 14, 1868. Available from: "Road Files," Santa Clara County Board of Supervisors.

13 McCaleb, *The San Jose Railroads: Centennial 1868-1968*, V.

14 McCaleb, *The San Jose Railroads: Centennial 1868-1968*, 1.

15 McCaleb, *The San Jose Railroads: Centennial 1868-1968*, 21.

16 McCaleb, *The San Jose Railroads: Centennial 1868-1968*, 7.

17 Colin Jung, "The San Jose Fisher Electric Road and its Glass Insulators."

18 Jung.

[19] Jung.

[20] Jung.

[21] Foote, 197-198.

[22] Arbuckle, 117.

[23] McCandless, 139.

[24] Richard L. Nailen, *Guardians of the Garden City: The History of the San José Fire Department* (San Jose: Smith and Mckay Printing Company, 2001), 157.

Residential Development

[1] Roscoe D. Wyatt, *Historic Names, Persons and Places in Santa Clara County* (San Jose: San Jose Chamber of Commerce, 1948), 40.

[2] Ralph Rambo, *Almost Forgotten* (Santa Clara: 1964), 27.

[3] Chester S. Lyman, *Around the Horn to the Sandwich Islands and California, 1845-1850* ed. Frederick J. Teggart (New Haven: Yale University Press, 1924), 217, 230-231.

[4] Clyde Arbuckle, *Santa Clara County Ranchos* (San Jose: Harlan-Young Press, 1968), 17.

[5] Wyatt, 27.

[6] Munro-Fraser 1881; Laffey 1981, Available from: "Historical Background of 941-945 The Alameda," Charlene Duval, 1999.

[7] Rockwell D. Hunt, "Houses that Came Around the Horn for the 'Alameda Gardens,'" *Overland Monthly*, Jan-June 1907, 210-215.

[8] H. S. Foote, *Pen Pictures from the Garden of the World of Santa Clara County California* (Chicago, IL: The Lewis Publishing Company, 1888).

[9] Hunt, 210-215.

[10] Gregory B. McCandless, "The Alameda of San Jose: A Historical Land Use and Development Study" (Masters thesis presented to the Department of Urban and Regional Planning, San Jose State University, 1988), 24.

[11] Foote, 360.

[12] Charlene Duval, 2006.

[13] "Second Polhemus House, Visual Inventory of Historic and Archaeological Sites," January 7, 1974. Inventory Number 1AP 233-CP.

[14] William F. James and George H. McMurry, *History of San Jose, California, Narrative and Biographical* (San Jose, CA: Smith Printing Company, 1933), 104.

[15] Charles S. McCaleb, *The San Jose Railroads: Centennial 1868-1968*, (Foothill Junior College District, 1968), 8.

[16] Helen W. Kennedy and Kinzie K. Veronica, *Vignettes of the Gardens of San Jose de Guadalupe* (San Jose: San Jose Garden Club, 1938), 19.

[17] Hunt, 210-215.

[18] McCandless, 49.

[19] Susan Fagalde Barnard, "The Alameda: One Hundred Seventy-nine Years of History," (Pioneer Papers of Santa Clara County, 1979), 4.

[20] McCaleb, *San Jose Railroads: Centennial 1868-1968*, 8.

[21] "Leet Estate---100 Years Later, a Change near," *San Jose Mercury News*, Jan. 13, 1952.

[22] G. H. McMurry, "City's Added Territory Has Past Crammed With Interest," *The Evening News*, San Jose, Dec. 14, 1925. California Room Newspaper Clippings.

[23] Edith Smith, "The William Square Clark Home" [sic], *San Jose Historical Museum Association*, Jan. 1987.

[24] *San Jose Mercury News*. Oct 1, 1955. History San José Newspaper Clippings.

[25] Patricia Loomis, *Signposts* (San Jose, CA: San Jose Historical Museum Association, 1982), 42.

[26] *Historical Atlas Map of Santa Clara County* (San Francisco: Thompson & West, 1876).

[27] G. H. McMurry, "City's Added Territory Has Past Crammed With Interest," *The Evening News*, San Jose, Dec. 14, 1925. California Room Newspaper Clippings.

[28] "S. J. Boasts Rare Old Mansion of…" *San Jose Mercury Herald and News.* History San José Newspaper Clippings.

[29] "Nostalgia: Wharf Builder's Home," *San Jose Mercury News,* Nov. 9, 1975.

[30] Gerry Reynolds, "Here's One Hidden By Magnolia Trees," *San Jose Mercury Herald,* Aug. 1946.

[31] Hunt, 210-215.

[32] Arbuckle, 1971. Available from: "Historical Background of 941-945 The Alameda," Charlene Duval, 1999.

[33] Book of Wills, B: 200-208, C: 27-33. Available from: "Historical Background of 941-945 The Alameda," Charlene Duval, 1999.

[34] Hunt, 210-215.

[35] Kennedy, 22.

[36] Hunt, 1907; Kennedy and Kinzie, 1938. Available from: "Historical Background of 941-945 The Alameda," Charlene Duval, 1999.

[37] David S. Jordan, *Days of a Man* (Yonkers-on-Hudson, NY: World Book Co., 1922), 129.

[38] H. S. Foote, *Pen Pictures from the Garden of the World of Santa Clara County California* (Chicago, IL: The Lewis Publishing Company, 1888), 621.

[39] J.M Guinn, *History and Biography* (Chicago, IL: The Chapman Publishing Co., 1904), 578.

[40] McCandless, 65.

[41] McCandless, 64.

[42] Adolf K. Placzek, *Macmillan Encyclopedia of Architects* vol. 3 (London: The Free Press, 1982), 238.

[43] Charlene Duval, A. Grady, and L. Dill, "The Dunne House," State of California—The Resources Agency, Department of Parks and Recreation, Nov. 23, 2001.

[44] Mary Jo Ignoffo, "Troubled Years," In *Reflections of the Past,* edited by Judith Henderson, 157. (Encinitas: Heritage Media Corporation, 1996).

[45] Clyde Arbuckle, *Clyde Arbuckle's History of San José* ed. Leonard McKay (San Jose: Smith and McKay Printing Company, 1986), 342.

[46] Arbuckle, 343.

[47] "Vengeance in San Jose," Crime Library, http://www.crimelibrary.com (accessed Sept. 12, 2006).

[48] J. B. Ridder, "San Jose Museum-To-Be Has Interesting Story," *San Jose Mercury News,* Dec. 14, 1952.

[49] Arbuckle, 118.

[50] McCandless, 30.

[51] Linda Dittes, "A Short History of The Rose Garden Area," Rose Garden Neighborhood Preservation Association, http://rgnpa.org/history.html (accessed Sept. 13, 2006).

[52] Public Works Records, Gen 514.

Education

[1] Loomis, 89.

[2] Rockwell D. Hunt, *History of the College of the Pacific, 1851-1951,* (Stockton: The College of the Pacific, 1951), 4.

[3] "Beginning of University of Pacific," California Room, Scrapbook L.

[4] Hunt, 8.

[5] Hunt, 19.

[6] Jack Douglas, *Historical Footnotes of Santa Clara Valley* (San Jose: San Jose Historical Museum Association, 1993), 51.

[7] Tanya Caldwell, "State's first colleges, by definition," *Los Angeles Times,* Sept. 12, 2006.

[8] Hunt, 15.

[9] Hunt, 11.

[10] *Historical Atlas Map of Santa Clara County,* (San Francisco: Thompson & West, 1876).

[11] Douglas, 52.

[12] Hunt, 27-28.

[13] Hunt, 12.

[14] Gregory B. McCandless, "The Alameda of San Jose: A Historical Land Use and Development Study" (Masters thesis presented to the Department of Urban and Regional Planning, San Jose State University, 1988), 27.

[15] "Landmark Nears End," *San Jose Mercury News*, sec 2, July 18, 1951.

[16] "Methodist College Makes Ready For Move to Stockton," *United Press*, Jan 14, 1922.

[17] Reginald R. Stuart and Grace D. Stuart, *Tully Knowles of Pacific* (Stockton: The College of the Pacific, 1956) 75.

[18] "About Bellarmine," Bellarmine College Preparatory, http://www2.bcp.org (accessed Sept. 16, 2006).

[19] "First English Language School In California, Taught by American Mrs. Olive M. Isbell, on Present Univ. of Santa Clara Campus," 1957. Santa Clara University Archives: Spearman Papers. n.d. Santa Clara University Archives: Spearman Papers.

[20] Audrey Youngs, "California's First American School Teacher: Olive Mann Isbell."

[21] Dorothy F. Regnery, *The Battle of Santa Clara* (San Jose: Smith and McKay Printing Company, 1978), 50.

[22] Regnery, 54.

[23] "Mustard Stalks Battle: 2 Cities Seek Plaque to Mark Conflict Site," *San Jose Mercury News*, Nov. 7, 1958. Santa Clara University Archives: Spearman Papers.

[24] "Battle of Mustard Stalks May Get a State Marker," *San Jose Mercury News*, Nov. 18 1858. Santa Clara University Archives: Spearman Papers.

[25] Mary A. Bowman. "The First American Teacher in California," *Land of Sunshine*, April 1895, 87.

[26] "First English Language School In California, Taught by American Mrs. Olive M. Isbell, on Present Univ. of Santa Clara Campus," 1957. Santa Clara University Archives: Spearman Papers.

The Alameda Attractions

[1] "Clubmen Recall 1901 Rose Event," *San Jose Mercury News*, April 13, 1926.

[2] Donald O. DeMers, Jr. and Ann M. Whitesell, *Santa Clara Valley: Images of the Past* (San Jose: San Jose Historical Museum Association, 1977), 52.

[3] Information about Fiesta de Las Rosas from: History San José, Festivals Folder and the California Room.

[4] Patricia Loomis, "Race Street Home of Early Fairs," *San Jose Mercury News*, Aug. 18, 1972.

[5] California Room Scraps collection.

[6] Eugene T. Sawyer, *History of Santa Clara County, California* (Los Angeles: Historic Record Company, 1922), 101.

[7] California Room Scraps collection.

[8] "Road Files," Santa Clara County Board of Supervisors.

[9] H. S. Foote, *Pen Pictures from the Garden of the World of Santa Clara County California* (Chicago, IL: The Lewis Publishing Company, 1888), 167.

[10] David Cherveny, F.R.C ,"Rosicrucian Park History, December 1927 to the Present," n.d.

Innovation and Industries

[1] George P. Connick, "John Joseph Montgomery, His Life In Brief," In Santa Clara County Pioneer Papers, 1973 (San Jose: California Pioneers of Santa Clara County, 1973).

[2] Ralph F. Rambo, *Adventure Valley: Pioneer Adventure in the Santa Clara Valley* (Santa Clara: 1970), 36-38.

[3] Eugene T. Sawyer, *History of Santa Clara County, California* (Los Angeles: Historic Record Company, 1922), 138.

[4] Gregory B. McCandless, "The Alameda of San Jose: A Historical Land Use and Development Study" (Masters thesis presented to the Department of Urban and Regional Planning, San Jose State University, 1988), 33.

[5] Eugene T. Sawyer, *History of Santa Clara County, California* (Los Angeles: Historic Record Company, 1922), 138-139.

[6] Glory Anne Laffey, "Calpak Manager's Office," Building, Structure, and Object Record, California Department of Parks and Recreation, 37.

[7] Helen Arbuckle, *San Jose's Women: Colonial Days to the 1970's, a Brief History* ed. Jim Arbuckle (San Jose: J. Arbuckle, 2002), 56-57.

[8] H. S. Foote, *Pen Pictures from the Garden of the World of Santa Clara County California* (Chicago, IL: The Lewis Publishing Company, 1888), 198.

[9] Joanne Grant, "Beer once went home in old lard buckets," *San Jose Mercury News*, Jan. 14, 1991.

[10] "Nostalgia: The Fredericksburg," *San Jose Mercury News*, July 14, 1974.

[11] "What's in a Bottle?" *California Today*, May 9, 1971.

[12] "Wieland's To Celebrate 100th Anniversary," *California Today*, May 14, 1952.

[13] Joanne Grant, "Beer once went home in old lard buckets," *San Jose Mercury News*, Jan 14, 1991.

[14] Richard L. Nailen, *Guardians of the Garden City: The History of the San José Fire Department* (San Jose: Smith and Mckay Printing Company, 2001), 164-165.

[15] Charlene Detlefs [Duval], "Flour Milling in Santa Clara County, 1840-1898." (Masters thesis presented to the Department of Social Science, San Jose State University, 1985).

[16] Frank L. Beach, "James Alexander Forbes 1804-1881: British Vice Consul in California, 1842-1856," (Masters thesis presented to the Faculty of the Department of History, University of San Francisco, Jan. 1957), 155-164.

[17] Glory Anne Laffey and Charlene Duval, "Historical background for Holy Cross Cemetery City of San Jose," Feb. 11, 1997.

[18] Harry Farrell, "Eberhard Tannery." *San Jose Mercury News*, Feb. 11, 1953.

The Last Willows

[1] "Ancient Mission Willows Will Be Rejuvenated," *San Jose Mercury News*, Mar. 15, 1932.

[2] "Uniform Planting of Alameda Trees Planned by City," *San Jose Mercury News*, Jan. 28, 1932.

[3] "State Expert to Aid Civic Tree Planting Plans," *San Jose Mercury News*, Feb. 19, 1932.

[4] "Three Historic Alameda Willows Marked, Blessed" *Mercury Herald*, May 5, 1934.

[5] Patricia Loomis, *Signposts* (San Jose, CA: San Jose Historical Museum Association, 1982), 12.

[6] Patricia Loomis, "Mystery of the missing willow tree," *San Jose Mercury News*, Nov. 11, 1982.

Historical Vignettes

Habana Cuba: Jack Douglas, *Historical Footnotes of Santa Clara Valley* (San Jose: San Jose Historical Museum Association, 1993), 5-10.

Picture on front cover: "Sketch of The Alameda," by Victor Perard, courtesy of Sourisseau Academy

Edited by Brandon Chau

Picture on back cover: "The Alameda, 1901." Oil painting by Charles Harmon, Santa Clara University Archives.

Sketch of the willow tree on the walking tour plaque by Allison M. Clark

Selected Bibliography

Arbuckle, Clyde. *Clyde Arbuckle's History of San Jose.* San Jose: Smith & McKay Printing Company, 1985.

Arbuckle, Clyde & Rambo, Ralph. *Santa Clara County Ranchos.* San Jose. Rosicrucian Press, 1968.

Bancroft, J.J. *History of California.* San Francisco. A.L. Bancroft Co., 1984.

Beach, Frank L. "James Alexander Forbes 1804-1881: British Vice Consul in California, 1842-1856." Masters thesis presented to the Faculty of the Department of History, University of San Francisco, Jan. 1957.

Cady, Theron G. "Tales of the San Francisco Peninsula." *Peninsula Life Magazine,* 1948, http://www.sfgenealogy.com/sanmateo/history/smcady_c.htm (accessed Sept. 12, 2006).

City of San Jose's Department of City Planning. *The Alameda,* April 1984.

Detlefs, Charlene. "Flour Milling in Santa Clara County, 1840-1898." Masters thesis presented to the Department of Social Science, San Jose State University, 1985.

Douglas, Jack. *Historical Footnotes of Santa Clara Valley.* San Jose: San Jose Historical Museum Association, 1993.

Engelhardt, Zephyrin. *The Holy Man of Santa Clara: Life, Virtues and Miracles of Fr. Magín Catalá, O.F.M..* San Francisco: J. H. Barry, 1909.

Foote, H.S. *Pen Pictures from the Garden of the World of Santa Clara County California.* Chicago: The Lewis Publishing Company, 1888.

Fox, Francis. *Land Grant to Landmark.* San Jose: Smith & McKay Printing Company, 1978.

Garcia, Lorie, George Giacomini, and Geoffrey Goodfellow. *A Place of Promise.* Edited by DiMarco Tony. Santa Clara, CA: City of Santa Clara, 2002.

Guinn, J.M. *History and Biography.* Chicago: The Chapman Publishing Co., 1904.

Hall, Frederic. *History of San Jose.* San Francisco: A.L. Bancroft & Co., 1871.

Hylkema, Mark G. *Archeological Investigations at the Third Location of Mission Santa Clara de Asis.* Oakland: Caltrans District Four Environmental Planning, 1995.

Ingraham, William K. *Early Days of My Episcopate.* Oakland: Biobooks, 1954.

James, William F., and George H. McMurry. *History of San Jose.* San Jose: Smith Printing Co., 1933.

Kennedy, Helen W and Kinzie K. Veronica. *Vignettes of the Gardens of San Jose de Guadalupe.* San Jose: San Jose Garden Club, 1938.

Loomis, Patricia. *Signposts.* San Jose: San Jose Historical Museum Association, 1982.

Loomis, Patricia. *Signposts II.* San Jose: San Jose Historical Museum Association, 1985.

Mars, Amaury. *Reminiscences of Santa Clara Valley and San Jose.* San Francisco: Mysell-Rollins Co., 1901.

McCaleb, Charles S. *Tracks, Tires & Wires.* Glendale: Interurban Press, 1981.

McCaleb, Charles S. *The San Jose Railroads Centennial 1868-1968.* Foothill Junior College District, 1968.

McCandless, Gregory B. *The Alameda of San Jose : a historical land use and development study.* Masters thesis presented to the Department of Urban and Regional Planning, San Jose State University, 1988.

Munro-Fraser, J. P. *History of Santa Clara County.* San Francisco: Alley, Bowen & Co., 1881.

Nailen, Richard L. *Guardians of the Garden City: The History of the San José Fire Department.* 2 ed. San Jose: Smith and Mckay Printing Company, 2001.

Payne, Stephen M. *Santa Clara County: Harvest of Change.* Northridge: Windsor Publications, 1987.
Rambo, Ralph. *Almost Forgotten.* Santa Clara: 1964.

Regnery, Dorothy F. *The Battle of Santa Clara.* San Jose: Smith and McKay Printing Co., 1978.

Rose, Bertha M. *The Women of Our Valley.* Vol.II. San Jose: 1956.

Sawyer, Eugene T. *History of Santa Clara County, California.* Los Angeles: Historic Record Company, 1922.

Shortridge, Charles M. Santa Clara County and its Resources, (Sunshine, Fruit and Flowers). San Jose: San Jose Mercury Publ., 1895.

Shoup, Laurence H and Randall T. Milliken. *Inigo of Rancho Posolmi : the life and times of a mission Indian.* Menlo Park: Ballena Press, 1999.

Spearman, Arthur D. *The Five Franciscan Churches of Mission Santa Clara.* Palo Alto: The National Press, 1963.

Thompson and West. *Historical Atlas of Santa Clara County.* San Francisco: Thompson and West, 1876.

Winther, Oscar Osburn. The Story of San Jose, 1777-1869. San Francisco: California Historical Society, 1935.

www.siliconvalleyhistory.org